A Parent's Guide to

The Childhood Years
of Jesus Christ

Instilling the 6 Attributes of the Christ Child
Into Your Children

Ultimate Goal Publications

Jasonville, Indiana

www.stayinthecastle.com

(812) 665-4375

Dedicated to my daughters
— Amanda, Hannah, and Tabitha —
remarkable women all three.

Table of Contents

Introduction

Soon after the publishing of my book, *The Teenage Years of Jesus Christ*, requests began to pour in for material that would help parents in the rearing of their children during the first twelve years. For those who have asked, here it is.

Ever wish there were practice children? You know, children God gives you to rear so that you can make your mistakes before you get your "real" ones. During the writing of this book, I have walked my baby girl down the wedding aisle. Her two older sisters have both been married for several years and have given us six grandchildren! It seems that about the time your children grow up and are leaving, you feel like you might now know enough to begin raising them.

I will warn you ahead of time that this book is not written by a perfect dad — nor have my wife and I raised perfect children. In the writing of this book, I sometimes was tempted to retitle it "Would've, Could've, Should've!" However, despite our many shortcomings, God has blessed us with some pretty amazing daughters. We could not love them more, or be more thankful for the women they have become.

So I offer this book, not to point you to me as an example of anything. Instead, as you will see, my goal is to point you to Christ. He is and should always be our ultimate example. From His childhood, I will give you a template for child rearing. If being like Jesus is really what this Christian life is about, then I hope this book helps you point your children in His direction.

May God bless you as you pursue the greatest of all callings — that of being a mom or a dad! And may He bless you with much wisdom for the task ahead.

— Jerry Ross

Part One

The Ultimate Goal,
and How to Get There!

Part One
Chapter 1

Put a Ladder in Your Dreams

All parents have dreams for their child — dreams of what you hope your child will become when he/she reaches adulthood. These dreams start the day a wife tells her husband that she is expecting. They escalate during the course of the pregnancy until they almost overwhelm you on that day in the delivery room when you first hold your own flesh and blood. There is so much you want for them; so much you want them to become. Having dreams for our children is important.

They are also well nigh worthless without a ladder. That's right, a ladder. You need to put a ladder in your dreams.

"And he dreamed a dream, and behold a ladder set up on the earth, and the top of it reached to heaven: and behold the angels of God ascending and descending on it." Genesis 28:12

Jacob also had a dream. He dreamed of Heaven and of the Lord, of angels and beauty; and reaching up from where he was to what he dreamed was a ladder. A ladder with rungs or steps. Each step of this ladder lifted him closer from *where* he dreamed to *what* he dreamed. He not only envisioned the supernatural, but he saw the steps that would take him there.

Dreams for your children do not come true by wishing them so. You need a ladder, or steps, to get them from where they are to what you want them to someday be.

Let me illustrate this for you by asking you to participate in a simple exercise. I would like you to write down ten characteristics that you hope will be deeply engrained into the personality of your child by the time he/she reaches the age of twelve. Maybe it would help to put it this way: if you were going to meet with your twelve-year-old child's teacher for a parent-teacher conference, and you asked the teacher for the ten most prominent character traits she observes in your child, what ten would you hope she would mention? Stop now and write these down.

Are you done? Now look carefully at that list and ask yourself this question, "As his parent, what plans do I have or what steps will I take to see to it that my child is trained to be what I dream for him to be? Do I have a ladder to go along with my dream?"

Every dream needs a ladder. The world will try to sell you a humanistic ladder that they say is strong enough and safe enough for your children to use. Look around at what is happening to the children who are being raised according to the world's standards of right and wrong. Daily we read of these young people plummeting to the ground, lives broken and ruined because they were climbing on a ladder made of rotting, unreliable wood.

God never gives us a command without giving us instruction, or steps, to help us fulfill His command. He does not just tell us what He wants us to be, but also tells us how to become what He wants us to be. The Bible provides both a dream *and* a ladder.

Instead of buying the world's flimsy, flawed ladder of humanism, let me suggest you use a ladder constructed from material that is solid and sturdy, time-tested and true. Have your children climb steps that are divinely inspired, steps constructed from the principles and precepts found in God's Word.

Give them a Bible ladder.

Part One
Chapter 2

The Parental Ladder

Let's turn the dreams we have for our children into realities. Are you ready? Below are the seven steps that make up our parental ladder. You may want to get out your list of the ten most important attributes that you wish to have engrained into your child's character by his twelfth birthday. Now consider the first attribute on your list -- whatever it may be -- as we introduce each step of our parental ladder.

Step One - Proper Evaluation
"Be thou diligent to know the state of thy flocks, and look well to thy herds." Proverbs 27:23

The first step is *proper evaluation*. First, we must look at each of our children and critique their progress thus far toward the desired Biblical goals we have set for them. As parents, sometimes it is difficult for us to separate ourselves emotionally when it comes to our children -- hard not to succumb to the two extremes. We tend to be either too generous because they are ours or too critical because they are ours! You are, however, the one best suited to evaluate your children because no one knows them better than you do.

It is a God-given mandate that we take the time to know their "state"! Remember, God has entrusted you with their upbringing. All children are ultimately His, each a gift to us for a short time to be reared for God's honor and glory. So jot down each attribute below, and on a scale of one to ten (one being non-existent and ten being near perfect!) rate the development of each of your children's character in the ten target areas on your list. Use the table below if you wish. List your ten attributes on the blanks provided and then circle the number that you feel is a true evaluation of your child's development in each of these areas.

1. _____ 1 2 3 4 5 6 7 8 9 10

2. _____ 1 2 3 4 5 6 7 8 9 10

3. _____ 1 2 3 4 5 6 7 8 9 10

4. _____ 1 2 3 4 5 6 7 8 9 10

5. _____ 1 2 3 4 5 6 7 8 9 10

6. _____ 1 2 3 4 5 6 7 8 9 10

7. _____ 1 2 3 4 5 6 7 8 9 10

8. _____ 1 2 3 4 5 6 7 8 9 10

9. _____ 1 2 3 4 5 6 7 8 9 10

10. _____ 1 2 3 4 5 6 7 8 9 10

If your child is still an infant or young toddler, it may be too soon to evaluate him. However, every parent, no matter the child's age, should revisit this evaluation sheet from time to time, either to begin recording or to update your child's progress.

Step Two - Pointed Prayer
"...ye have not, because ye ask not." James 4:4b

The second step in the parental ladder is *specific and pointed prayer*. In order for us to see the improvements in our children's development, we must get God's help. Thank goodness for the Throne of Grace! There is One who loves your children more than you do, and He sits in Heaven wanting to help you; anxious to hear your requests. Allow the above evaluation sheet to become your personal prayer list! Ask God for His help as you seek to develop godly characteristics into your child's makeup.

Step Three - Parental Modeling
"My son, give me thine heart, and let thine eyes observe my ways." Proverbs 23:26

Parenting is not for sissies!!! Nothing will bring you face to face with your own shortcomings faster than rearing children. I don't know about you, but often I have been in the process of correcting one of my children in some area of her attitude or behavior, and have had the sweet Holy Spirit of God softly whisper into my mind, "Maybe before you correct her, you ought to take a hard look at yourself in that same area!"

The next step up the ladder involves some soul-searching on our part. We must take the same evaluation sheet and fill it out again -- not with our children in mind, but instead with ourselves as the subject of examination. Again, beware of the two extremes! Often we are either too easy on ourselves or too hard on ourselves. The best chance we have of completing a proper examination is to enlist the help of the Holy Spirit of God. I am reminded of David's sincere, heart-felt plea to God.

"Search me, O God, and know my heart: try me and know my thoughts: and see if there be any wicked way in me, and lead me in the way everlasting." Psalms 139:23-24

Why is this step so critical? Character is learned more by observation than any other way. One man said, "Excellent character is as much caught as taught". Solomon instructed his son, *"...give me thine heart, and let thine eyes observe my ways"*. Rest assured, our children are watching us! If we dream for our children to be honest, then we must be honest. If we dream for them to have a heart for God, then our hearts must burn with the desire to know Him better!

Step Four - Patient Instruction
"My son, hear the instruction of thy father, and forsake not the law of thy mother." Proverbs 1:8

The next step involves *patient, consistent, verbal instruction.* Many parents make use of a daily family altar or family devotions. Although this is certainly noble, I am reminded that verbal instruction must never be limited to a few minutes a day. Notice God's instruction to the parents concerning the law of Moses.
"And these words, which I command thee this day, shall be in thine heart: and thou shalt teach them diligently unto thy children, and shalt talk of them when thou sittest in thine house, and when thou walkest by the way, and when thou liest down, and when thou risest up." Deuteronomy 6:6-7
Some of the sweetest times I have had with my daughters were when God allowed me to share some truth with them in the course of everyday life. God will open up wonderful opportunities for us to impart His wisdom to each of our children if we stay in tune with the Holy Spirit. Years from now — long after we have gone to Heaven — the important, real-life spiritual lessons we taught them should still be a guiding force in their lives.

Step Five - Practical Training
"Train up a child in the way he should go; and when he is old, he will not depart from it." Proverbs 22:6

Teaching is verbal instruction. Training is supervised, practical experience. Teaching speaks to the head, but training teaches the hands. Training is absolutely necessary if a child is to master a skill. A mother can sit at the kitchen table and verbally instruct her daughter on the fine art of making chocolate-chip cookies (in my opinion, an absolute necessity if she will one day make a fine wife!). However, that young lady will never become a proficient baker until she rolls up her sleeves and, under the tutelage of a mother's patient and watchful eye, begins to mix the ingredients herself.

Verbal teaching has to be married to practical training. Their offspring will be children with knowledge and understanding. Knowledge comes from hearing how, but understanding is only achieved by doing. A lack of practical training has robbed an entire generation of something called "common sense".

A father once lamented to me, "I don't know what is wrong with my son! I have told him a dozen times how to do that task and he still doesn't get it! He seems to have no common sense!" My answer was simple and Biblical.

"You can tell him a dozen times more, but until you *show* him and then let him do it, patiently instructing him and correcting him as needed, he will never master the skill necessary to accomplish the task."

One man shared with me this simple formula. "You watch me do it. You help me do it. I'll help you do it. I'll watch you do it!"

Step Six - Praise and Reward
"The wicked worketh a deceitful work: but to him that soweth righteousness shall be a sure reward." Proverbs 11:18

I believe in praising a child when he has done well. I believe in rewarding a child who has excelled. I believe in it because God believes in it. Again and again in the Bible, God promises blessings upon those who obediently serve Him. He talks in His Word of crowns that await us at the judgment seat as well as opportunities to rule and reign with Him if we are found faithful. God is the ultimate example of a good Father!

Too often, as parents, we are quick with correction for shortcomings, but slow to praise a job well done. As our children exhibit excellent character, we should be liberal with verbal praise and generous with tangible rewards.

Step Seven - Purposeful Correction
"The rod and reproof give wisdom, but a child left to himself bringeth his mother to shame." Proverbs 29:15

Teaching and training alone do not insure that a child will develop wisdom. I have often said to my young adult class, "Teaching wisdom to your children does not necessarily make them wise, but it will make them choose between wisdom and foolishness." When a child has been taught and trained, yet purposefully chooses to do wrong, God places the responsibility to correct that child firmly upon the shoulders of his parents. However, to be effective, it must be carried out Biblically and purposefully. We will cover this step in more depth later.

Now let's place the steps together in front of us so that we can clearly view our Parental Ladder.

Step One: Proper Evaluation
Step Two: Pointed Prayer
Step Three: Parental Modeling
Step Four: Patient Instruction
Step Five: Practical Training
Step Six: Praise and Reward
Step Seven: Purposeful Correction

The purpose of this book is to point you to our precious Savior. Jesus, at age twelve, was a remarkable young man. Together, we will discover and examine the six powerful and unique character traits that we see clearly defined in His words and actions.

Part One
Chapter 3

Christ's Childhood

In this book, we will examine six character traits which Christ possessed as a twelve-year-old child. There is a chapter dedicated to each one. Add these attributes to your list of ten target attributes if they are not already there. As a matter of fact, make them the first six on your list. *The ultimate goal of the Christian life is to be like Jesus.* The ultimate goal for the Christian parent is to train Christ-like characteristics into your children.

"My little children, of whom I travail in birth again until Christ be formed in you." Galatians 4:19

What a verse! I was present in the delivery room when my wife gave birth to each of our three daughters. There are no words that can describe the extremity of her physical, mental, and emotional effort during her hours of labor. Travail is certainly an accurate word for the birthing process. Yet God states in His Word that we should use the same intensity of effort to mold Christ-likeness into our children.

What are the six attributes of the twelve-year-old Christ-child? How can we put into use our *Parental Ladder* to help our children possess these same attributes? First, allow me to present an overview of the childhood of Jesus Christ.

A Boy Named Jesus

"And the child grew..." Luke 2:40

"...they found him in the temple, sitting in the midst of the doctors, both hearing them and asking them questions." Luke 2:46

"And Jesus increased in wisdom and stature..." Luke 2:52

Jesus grew? Jesus needed to be taught? Jesus increased in wisdom? If Jesus was indeed God (and He was!), how can these statements be true?

Although Jesus was God the Son, He chose -- when coming to earth and taking on the form of flesh -- not to access His divine knowledge and supernatural power during His growing up years. He did, of course, retain His divine nature. Jesus did not have man's sin nature, but He did accept the physical, mental, and spiritual limitations imposed on all children born into this world. Physically, He had to grow and develop. Mentally, He had to study and learn. Even spiritually, He slowly increased in strength. Jesus came to fulfill the will of His Father and He accomplished this, not with the supernatural power available to Him as the Son of God, but in the power available to every man - the power of the Holy Spirit. Notice these verses:

*John 5:19, "Then answered Jesus and said unto them, Verily, verily, I say unto you, **The Son can do nothing of himself, but what he seeth the Father do**: for what things soever he doeth, these also doeth the Son likewise."*

*John 5:30, "**I can of mine own self do nothing**: as I hear, I judge: and my judgment is just; because I seek not mine own will, but **the will of the Father** which hath sent me."*

*Luke 4:1 "And Jesus **being full of the Holy Ghost** returned from Jordan, and was led **by the Spirit** into the wilderness,"*

*Luke 4:14, "And Jesus returned **in the power of the Spirit...**"*

*Matthew 12:28, "But if I cast out devils **by the Spirit of God**, then the kingdom of God is come unto you."*

This choice to be directed solely by the will of the Father and perform wholly in the power of the Spirit did not make Jesus any less divine in His nature. He chose to live as He would ask us to live, to access only those things available to us today. By doing this, He became our Supreme Example.

I have spent time explaining this because I think it is interesting to note that Jesus had to learn and live and grow in the same way our children do. Jesus did so without ever sinning, but that does not mean that He was never tested, tried, frustrated, challenged or misunderstood.

*"For we have not an high priest which cannot be touched with the **feelings of our infirmities**; but was in all points tempted like as we are, **yet without sin**." Hebrews 4:14*

He was touched with all of the feelings of our infirmities. He experienced every childhood frustration and challenge. He was a perfect Child being raised in an imperfect world. Consider these Bible facts concerning the circumstances of His upbringing.

Jesus was a hunted child.

Soon after Christ's birth, when Herod discovered that the wise men had not returned to tell him where he could find the newly born King of the Jews, Herod decreed the slaughter of all Hebrew children two years old and under in Bethlehem and the surrounding coasts. Had it not been for a divine warning and Joseph's immediate obedience, Christ would have been killed. So great was the manhunt conducted by this murderous and insanely insecure Roman ruler that God commanded Joseph to leave the country, to flee to Egypt in order to protect the Child's life.

Because of this, Jesus' first few formative years were spent in a foreign land among people of unfamiliar customs and a strange tongue. Israelites were looked upon with disdain in Egypt, and His family was no doubt mistreated from time to time. Joseph would have had to earn a living in an environment where the best jobs went to the men of that country. At a time when he should have been establishing the foundations of a permanent home and a successful business, he instead found himself struggling to meet his family's needs.

It is wonderful to think how God provided for the family during these years. Remember the three wise men and their gifts? The gold, frankincense, and myrrh no doubt were used frugally by Joseph to help finance the family's existence during these years on the run.

Even after Herod's death, when God sent an angel to tell Joseph that he could now return with his family to Israel, that same angel returned again with a warning to turn aside into Galilee and not return to Judea. The danger lingered still because Herod's son, Archelaus, reigned in his father's stead. So Joseph and Mary quietly made their home in Nazareth, being careful not to mention too much of their past — where they had come from and why they had moved.

I have often wondered at how seemingly insecure Christ's childhood must have been. As any mother would, Mary no doubt warned Him against talking to strangers and sharing who He was or where He came from. Maybe she gave Him instructions as to what to do and where to hide should any Roman soldiers find their way into the region. How would any small boy react to such things?

Jesus was a child who lived with undeserved guilt.

At some point, Jesus no doubt learned of the slaughter of the young children of Bethlehem and all the coasts round about shortly after His birth — a slaughter that was the result of the soldiers seeking Him. I wonder at the guilt and personal responsibility that He felt over these murders.

Maybe at some point He came to Mary and asked, "Why did so many have to die because of me? Why are they dead and I am alive?"

You might say, "But He was God. He understood what was happening."

He grew. He increased. He learned. Remember, He was touched by the *feelings* of our infirmities. He was both man and God. He felt what any boy His age would have felt, short of sin.

Jesus was raised in a poor home.

This was not because Joseph did not work hard. The Bible tells us enough about Joseph for us to understand that he was a remarkable man. How could he be anything less? After all, it was God who chose him as the father figure for Jesus. (Later in the book, we have devoted an entire chapter to this unique and godly man.) We do know that he and Mary started out with little or nothing. I know this for two reasons. Had he been well to do, housing would have been found in Bethlehem for his family. I can assure you, no people of means were spending nights housed in a stable. Also, when Jesus was brought to the temple eight days after His birth to be circumcised and dedicated to the Lord, His parents brought a sacrifice of two clean birds. In Leviticus chapter twelve, a family was commanded to bring a lamb for sacrifice when dedicating their first born son to God, or two turtledoves or pigeons if they could not afford a lamb. Joseph and Mary's financial situation only allowed for them to bring two clean birds.

Out of necessity, Joseph moved his family around a lot. As already stated, he had to live for some time in Egypt and then in a part of Israel far from where their relatives lived. Joseph worked hard, yet his family lived without most of the materialistic advantages of his day. Jesus grew up in a family that knew what it was like to struggle and to live without most of the niceties of life.

Jesus was a child who lived under the spotlight of supernatural expectations.

Family came to visit. Mary and Joseph made friends. One way or another, I'm sure some of the astounding stories surrounding the conception, birth, and life of this boy were whispered amongst those who lived around Him. The stories of His immaculate conception, of the shepherds and their celestial visitors, of dark men from the far east and the extravagant gifts they bore, retold accounts of the declarations of Simeon the priest and Anna the prophetess weaved their way through the surrounding countryside. Hushed speculation about His future as a great prophet no doubt led to grandeur debates concerning the possibility that He was, indeed, the Messiah. Small towns are small towns. Such stories and speculation circulated the small village of Nazareth. The level of expectation that He was subjected to was, at times, staggering. As a child, that is a lot to carry.

Jesus was a child who lived under the spotlight of questionable legitimacy.

For those who were prone to doubt these stories or simply prefer dark, evil speculation, there were other rumors to banter about. Perhaps the child was not the result of a miraculous conception but of a scandalous, premarital affair. Children of that day were as prone to cruelty toward their peers as children are today. I wonder how many times He was laughed at or called a "bastard". We know that these rumors existed because, even as an adult, the Pharisees implied that Jesus was the product of fornication.

"...We be not born of fornication; we have one Father, even God." John 8:41

I share these truths with you because it is important for us to realize that Jesus was not reared in a perfect environment. He did not have perfect parents. But He did have parents who loved Him and helped Him develop strong character. Despite some very difficult circumstances, at the age of twelve we find in Him six important and vital character traits. These provided the foundation for all that He was to accomplish.

Six attributes of Christ at Age 12

"And the child grew, and waxed strong in spirit, filled with wisdom: and the grace of God was upon him." Luke 2:40

"And it came to pass, that after three days they found him in the temple, sitting in the midst of the doctors, both hearing them, and asking them questions. And all that heard him were astonished at his understanding and answers." Luke 2:46-47

"And he said unto them, How is it that ye sought me? wist ye not that I must be about my Father's business?" Luke 2:49

These verses give us insight to the character of Christ at age twelve. Notice these six attributes that were firmly instilled into His personality at this still tender age.

1. Strength of Spirit
2. Godly Wisdom
3. Divine Graciousness
4. Hunger for Knowledge
5. Depth of Understanding
6. Clarity of Purpose

What an amazing list! Read them again and think how you would feel if folks recognized these as the strongest character traits of your child at age twelve.

Part Two

The Six Attributes
of a Child Named Jesus

Part Two
Chapter 1

Strength of Spirit

When you buy a car, it comes with an owner's manual. It also comes with a warning: ***"Before Operating Vehicle, Completely Read the Owner's Manual"***. The owner's manual is written by the company who made the car, and it outlines in great detail the major parts of the vehicle as well as a list of instructions for its care and maintenance.

Children also come with an owner's manual. It is called the Bible. This manual is written by the Creator of your children. It also carefully outlines the major parts and provides maintenance principles for each part.

God Originally Created Man a Triune Creature

God created Adam and Eve in His image. Of all living things created by God, only mankind is a triune creature. It is what made us unique.

"And the very God of peace sanctify you wholly; and I pray God your whole spirit and soul and body be preserved blameless unto the coming of our Lord Jesus Christ." I Thessalonians 5:23

Man was originally created with a spirit, a soul, and a body. God warned Adam that the consequences of disobedience to God (transgression of His laws) was death.

"And the LORD God took the man, and put him into the garden of Eden to dress it and to keep it. And the LORD God commanded the man, saying, Of every tree of the garden thou mayest freely eat: But of the tree of the knowledge of good and evil, thou shalt not eat of it: for in the day that thou eatest thereof thou shalt surely die." Gen. 2:15-17

The Spirit of Man Died in Eden

You cannot strengthen something that is dead. There is noth-ing more futile than trying to develop spirituality without a new-born spirit.

"Wherefore as by one man sin entered into the world, and

death by sin, and so death passed upon all men, for that all have sinned." Romans 5:12

When Adam and Eve ate the forbidden fruit, their spirit died. Their soul did not die and their body did not die. Sin brought spiritual death (literally the death of our spirit) upon mankind. Had he and Eve not accepted the "coats of skins" (representing the blood sacrifice) they would have eventually died physically and then suffered eternal separation from God.

The Spirit of Man is Reborn at Salvation

Thank God for the blood! Because Jesus shed His blood on Calvary's cross, salvation is available to all men. The Holy Spirit regenerates the spirit of a man at the moment of true conversion. That which was dead as a result of sin is now brought back to life.

"Jesus answered, Verily, verily, I say unto thee, Except a man be born of water and of the Spirit, he cannot enter into the kingdom of God. That which is born of the flesh is flesh; and that which is born of the Spirit is spirit." John 3:5-6

Notice that, in the above verse, the first time the word *spirit* appears in this phrase it is capitalized, and the second time it is not. The Holy Spirit literally rebirths our dead spirit. Once again, man can become the triune creature he was originally created to be.

Your Child's Spirit Cannot Be Strengthened Until He is Born Again

As a parent, your first order of business is to do all you can to help your child understand both the Gospel and his need to receive Jesus Christ as his own personal Savior. The Bible teaches us that, before anyone can be saved, several divine ingredients must be in place.

Ingredients That Lead To A True Conversion

Salvation is the result of grace and faith. There must, however, be a clear understanding of some basic Bible doctrine in order for this faith to be activated. Remember, *"...faith cometh by hearing, and hearing by the word of God." Romans 10:17*

Let me share with you the five ingredients that lead to a true conversion.

1. Holy Spirit conviction of our sinful state

"Nevertheless I tell you the truth; It is expedient for you that I go away: for if I go not away, the Comforter will not come unto you; but if I depart, I will send him unto you. And when he is come, he will reprove the world of sin, and of righteousness, and of judgment:" John 16:7-8

No one has ever gotten saved who was not first willing to acknowledge his own personal sinfulness. No one has ever gotten saved who did not see that his sin places him in a state of condemnation before God. If there is no Holy Spirit conviction, there is no true conversion.

As parents, we determine our children's attitudes toward personal sin in two ways:

a) In the example we set in dealing with our own personal sin. Some children are not getting saved simply because they have been reared in an environment where no one ever takes personal responsibility for their sin or, if they do, there is no personal sorrow to accompany that responsibility. Our wrong doings and shortcomings are laughed off or excused away. They see mom and dad sin, then see them blame others instead of accepting personal responsibility. The children then begin to mimic what they see.

b) In the attitude and action we take when dealing with our child's sins. Biblical discipline teaches a child the act of true repentance. If instead of disciplining our children when they do wrong, we defend them or make excuses for them, we condition them against accepting personal responsibility and as a result, condition them against getting saved.

2. The Drawing Power of God

Notice Christ's words concerning the necessity of the drawing power of God.

"No man can come to me, except the Father which hath sent me draw him: and I will raise him up at the last day." John 6:44

No man! Without the drawing of the Father, no man is saved. The word *draw* literally means *to urge forward.* I share this with you because, as parents, we have a natural desire to see our children saved at the earliest possible age. If we are not careful, *we urge* them to a decision instead of allowing the Holy Spirit to bring real divine conviction, and the Father to place upon them a divine urgency. Getting our children to agree to repeat a prayer does not save them.

No one knows your child as well as you do. Watch for a divine urging. When the conviction of the Holy Spirit is accompanied by the urging of the Father, a young person is ready to receive the Gospel.

3. A Clear Understanding of Who Jesus Is

A young person must believe that Jesus is the Son of God. Placing your faith in a "good man" or a "holy prophet" or a "created angel" does not save you. The deity of Christ is an essential doctrine for salvation.

"Who is a liar but he that denieth that Jesus is the Christ? He is antichrist, that denieth the Father and the Son. Whosoever denieth the Son, the same hath not the Father: (but) he that acknowledgeth the Son hath the Father also." I John 2:22-23

"Beloved, believe not every spirit, but try the spirits whether they are of God: because many false prophets are gone out into the world. Hereby know ye the Spirit of God: Every spirit that confesseth that Jesus Christ is come in the flesh is of God: And every spirit that confesseth not that Jesus Christ is come in the flesh is not of God: and this is that spirit of antichrist, whereof ye have heard that it should come; and even now already is it in the world." I John 4:1-3

Most children accept that Jesus is the Son of God simply and by faith. A person who does not accept the doctrine of the deity of Christ cannot be saved.

4. A Clear Understanding of the Gospel Story

"For I am not ashamed of the gospel of Christ: for it is the power of God unto salvation to everyone that believeth; to the Jew first, and also to the Greek." Romans 1:16

The Gospel is the power of God unto salvation. As Dr. Lee Roberson said time and time again, "It's dynamite!" What is the Gospel message?

"Moreover, brethren, I declare unto you the gospel which I preached unto you, which also ye received, and wherein ye stand; By which also ye are saved, if ye keep in memory what I preached unto you, unless ye have believed in vain. For I delivered unto you first of all that which I also received, how that Christ died for our sins according

to the scriptures; And that he was buried, and that he rose again the third day according to the scriptures." I Corinthians 15:1-4

The word "gospel" means "good news". The Gospel message is simple and clear. Don't complicate it! Christ died for our sins, was buried, and rose again the third day. Teach your children the simple story of the substitutionary death and bodily resurrection of Jesus. Make sure they are in a church where the Gospel is presented plainly and often. They must, by faith, believe the Gospel in order to be saved.

"That if thou shalt confess with thy mouth the Lord Jesus, and shalt believe in thine heart that God hath raised him from the dead, thou shalt be saved." Romans 10:9

5. An Act of Simple Faith

"And Jesus called a little child unto him, and set him in the midst of them. And said, Verily I say unto you, Except ye be converted, and become as little children, ye shall not enter into the kingdom of heaven." Matthew 18:2-3

Children can and do experience true conversion. I have heard some preachers suggest that young children cannot be saved; that they must achieve some level of adult maturity before they can truly be converted. The Bible teaches the exact opposite. Jesus told the adults that unless they were willing to become like "little children", they would not enter the kingdom of Heaven.

Faith is believing without seeing. A child has an enormous capacity for simple faith. They tend to believe very easily that Jesus was Christ, the Messiah. Most children easily believe the Gospel story without question . If your child understands the Gospel and you see in him an acknowledgement of his sin accompanied by true repentance -- a desire to turn to Christ -- brought on by obvious Holy Spirit conviction and fueled by a divine urging of the Father, he is ready to be saved!

When he does get saved, remember, your child now has a spirit. Your job is not over. You now are responsible to see that his spirit is properly developed — that he waxes "strong in spirit" for the glory of God.

Your Child's Spirit is the Part of Him that Communicates Directly with God

This is important for us to remember. Because of this, we

should strive to develop and strengthen this new-born, divine part of our children.

"God is a Spirit: and they that worship him **must worship him in spirit** and in truth." John 4:24

"**The Spirit itself beareth witness with our spirit,** that we are the children of God." Romans 8:16

"But as it is written, eye hath not seen, nor ear heard, neither have entered into the heart of man, the things which God hath prepared for them that love him. But God hath revealed them by his Spirit: for the Spirit searcheth all things, yea, the deep things of God. For what man knoweth the things of a man, save the spirit of man which is in him? even so the things of God knoweth no man, but the Spirit of God. **Now we have received not the spirit of the world, but the spirit which is of God; that we might know the things that are freely given to us of God.**" I Corinthians 2:9-12

After your child is born again, he is indwelt by the Holy Spirit of God. The Holy Spirit regenerates the spirit of your child at the moment of new birth, and he becomes the triune creature that God always intended man to be. Notice that a saved child now consists of three parts:

a) a spirit (reborn by the Spirit)
b) a soul (mind, heart, and will)
c) a body (our flesh)

Before he was saved, he could not communicate with God. Why? Because God is a Spirit and He communicates to man through man's spirit. That is why an unsaved person cannot have fellowship with God. That is why an unsaved person cannot worship God and cannot discern the hidden meaning of the Scriptures. Why? Because he can only approach the Bible on a fleshly, intellectual, or emotional level. The Holy Spirit is the only One who can open to us the Word of God and He does so through communication with our spirit.

"Which things also we speak, not in words which man's wisdom teacheth, but which the Holy Ghost teacheth; comparing spiritual things with spiritual. **But the natural man receiveth not the things of the Spirit of God:** for they are foolishness unto him: neither can he know them, **because they are spiritually discerned**." I Cor. 2:13-14

The Holy Spirit is our divine Tutor. As we study the Scriptures, He communicates to us through our spirit -- not our intellect, not our emotions, and certainly not our flesh. These parts of man are natural, not spiritual, and the natural man cannot receive "the things of the Spirit of God".

The Development of our Children Should Promote Their Spirit to Its Rightful Place of Prominence

"It is the spirit that quickeneth; the flesh profiteth nothing. The words I speak unto you, they are spirit and they are life." John 6:63

*"And the child (John the Baptist) grew, **and waxed strong in spirit**, and was in the deserts till the day of his shewing unto Israel."* Luke 1:80

*"And the child (Jesus) grew, **and waxed strong in spirit**, filled with wisdom: and the grace of God was upon him."* Luke 2:40

*"For this cause I bow my knees unto the Father of our Lord Jesus Christ, of whom the whole family in heaven and earth is named, that he would grant you according to the riches of his glory, **to be strengthened with might by his Spirit in the inner man**."* Ephesians 3:14-16

John the Baptist was proclaimed by Jesus as the greatest prophet ever born. Perhaps one of the reasons was this: as a child he waxed strong in spirit. The Bible does not comment on how physically strong he was, or how high his IQ, or even whether or not he was especially talented or gifted. The Bible emphasizes that his spirit waxed strong.

The same is true of Jesus as a child. He is our supreme example! If you get nothing else out of this book, please understand what the Bible teaches here. The greatest mistake Christian parents are making in the rearing of their children is the exaltation of their child's physical, emotional, and intellectual development and the utter neglect of the child's spiritual development. While athleticism is exalted almost to the point of worship, spiritual strength is neglected and often ridiculed. Homework is required, yet personal devotions often are not even encouraged, let alone required. The Bible is not against the development and strengthening of a child's body, intellect or emotions. It does, however, teach us that these things should never supersede the importance of strengthening his spirit.

When the parts of a child are not in the right order, problems arise. Let's look at three possible arrangements of a child's spirit, soul, and body and examine the results of each.

Strength of the Spirit: The Spiritual Man
Holy Spirit>Spirit>Soul>Body

Remember, the Holy Spirit communicates only with the spirit of man. The spirit, if it is the strongest, then controls the soul. This produces a child who has Spirit-led, spirit-controlled thoughts, feelings and will.

Strength of the Body: The Athlete/Beauty Queen
Body>Soul>Spirit>Holy Spirit

This is the priority scheme of many Christian parents and children in this current Laodicean age. Christian schools, youth programs, and children's programs -- even within our fundamental churches -- promote (by their scheduling, actions, and rewards) the development of a child's flesh far above any other aspect of their divine make-up. This is the order of the carnal Christian. To be *carnal* simply means to be "fleshly". The flesh is fed, coddled, exercised, promoted, and developed at the expense of everything else. It is the mistake of a Christian school who has sports programs galore but no youth soul winning program. Ball practice or a game of one kind or another consume the schedule, but most involved have not spent ten minutes reading their Bible, not ten minutes in prayer and have not witnessed to a lost person in weeks.

The result is that the flesh grows strong and the spirit is demoted to last in importance. Because the Holy Spirit communicates with man's spirit, He is also shoved to the end. Then we wonder why so many of our Christian teens get involved in sins of the flesh. Why is it that the Christian schools who - by schedule if not words - promote sports over spirituality also have the greatest problem with immorality amongst their teens? Why is it those schools and youth groups produce so few preachers, full-time Christian workers, or young people whose sole purpose in life is finding and achieving the will of God?

The answer is simple: you will reap the rewards of what you

promote! *"For he that soweth to his flesh shall of the flesh reap corruption..."* (Galatians 6:8) We say we want spiritual young people, but we set up a program where the applause and accolades go to those who spend the bulk of their time developing the strength of their flesh.

Strength of the Soul: The Intellectual/Philosopher
Soul>Body>Spirit>Holy Spirit

One of the hats I wear at our church is that of a Christian School Administrator. I tell you this because I want you to understand that in the past eighteen years, I have spent an incredible amount of time working to improve the academic standards in our school. I work relentlessly to see to it that a child who attends our school gets a quality education. Having said that, let me add this: I am a hundred times more concerned where a young person is spiritually than where he is academically. If I had to make a choice, I would take the student who has a "C" average and is making an "A" in godliness, than a straight "A" student who is failing Practical Holiness 101. Shame on us for emphasizing the development of our children's minds over and above the development of their spirits.

Our churches are filled with young people who are book smart and obedience dumb. They had above average SAT and ACT scores, but, after they graduated they "SAT" down spiritually and we are still waiting for them to "ACT" godly. You can be an academic genius and a spiritual idiot. Our state colleges and universities are full of them! No one should ever get too smart to serve. If you are too educated to humble yourself at an altar during an invitation, follow your pastor, work a bus route, volunteer for the nursery, or go soul winning, then you have educated yourself beyond usefulness. You have accumulated knowledge but have failed miserably in the principal thing, the development of practical spirituality.

Why the Flood?

We see the demise of the Spiritual man, and the rise of the Athlete/Beauty Queen and Intellectual/Philosopher in the years leading up to the flood.

"And it came to pass, when men began to multiply on the face

of the earth, and daughters were born unto them, That the sons of God saw the daughters of men that they were fair; and they took them wives of all which they chose. And the LORD said, My spirit shall not always strive with man, for that he also is flesh: yet his days shall be an hundred and twenty years. There were giants in the earth in those days; and also after that, when the sons of God came in unto the daughters of men, and they bare children to them, the same became mighty men which were of old, men of renown. And GOD saw that the wickedness of man was great in the earth, and that every imagination of the thoughts of his heart was only evil continually." Genesis 6:1-5

Outlined in these Scriptures are the four main segments of the human race:

1. **The sons of God** - These were the descendants of Seth, a spiritual civilization who worshipped and served Jehovah God.

2. **The daughters of men** - The civilization that was created by the descendants of Cain who "went out" from the presence of God.

3. **Mighty men** - A description of the offspring of the sons of God and the daughters of men, meaning men famous for physical strength and athletic prowess.

4. **Men of renown** - Another description of the offspring of the sons of God and the daughters of men, meaning men famous for their great knowledge and intellect.

Here, briefly, is the story. Two civilizations emerged from Adam and Eve. The descendants of Cain created a civilization where God was excluded. The descendants of Seth, on the other hand, created a civilization where Jehovah God was honored and worshipped. For many generations, these two civilizations had little or no contact.

At some point, they grew and expanded to the point where there began to be increased contact. The young men, who were descendants of Seth, began to notice the young ladies from Cain's lineage. They began to pursue them because of one stated reason: they were fair to look upon — appealing to the eyes and flesh. Years ago, Cain's civilization had left behind decency and virtue. Like many young women of today's world, they had been raised with the dangerous notion that the way to attract men was through immodesty and seduction. They wore less, but they were also worth far less.

God's reaction to His children marrying the worldly inhabitants of earth was anger. (It is still His reaction today!) He was so angry that He immediately shortened the average life span of mankind to 120 years. (That may still seem like a lot of years, but remember, Adam lived to be 930 years old. If we use his age as a benchmark, God reduced man's lifespan by 87%!)

The offspring of these unholy unions were two main types of men: the Athlete/Warrior and the Intellectual/Philosopher. Instead of having children who were known for their spiritual strength and loyalty to Jehovah God, now we have the world's new definition of greatness. In this new society created through compromise, a person now was considered a success if he was physically powerful or appealing, or if he was a master of the world's definition of wisdom and genius.

Notice that this new emphasis did not lead to a better world. The next verse chronicles for us the result of the exaltation of the soul and flesh, and the neglect of the spirit. *"And God saw the wickedness of man was great in the earth, and that every imagination of the thoughts of his heart was only evil continually. And it repented the Lord that he had made man on the earth, and it grieved him at his heart." Genesis 6:5-6*

It is the same today! Why do we live in such a wicked world? Because we have, for the last many generations, forsaken our spiritual heritage, and instead have fallen down and worshipped the golden calf of humanism. The world's heroes are the sports stars or the Hollywood actors or actresses. Strength and beauty define one aspect of success. Academic or financial genius the other. If you are rich, smart, handsome, beautiful, strong or powerful, then you are considered great. When we read Christ's prophetic words found in Matthew 24:37, we cannot help but realize that He is soon to appear. *"But as the days of Noe were, so shall also the coming of the Son of man be."*

I overheard two ladies in front of me in one of our local store's check-out lanes. One was bragging about her son receiving an athletic scholarship to the state university. The other, not to be outdone, began to brag about the fact that her daughter had received an academic scholarship to a well know Ivy League school. I could not resist interrupting them, and, just to see their reaction, told them my daughter was planning on attending a Bible college when she graduated. They didn't seem the least bit impressed! That's all right. I didn't expect them to be. To be honest, I wasn't too impressed with their stories either.

The world has defined greatness to include achievements in either physical beauty or strength, or achievements in intellectual endeavors. What grieves God is that this same measuring stick is also being used in the church. Many Christian parents would be more proud of their children if they became famous in this world, or made a lot of money, than if they surrendered their lives to serve God.

Using Our Parental Ladder to Develop in our Children Strength of Spirit

Step One - Proper Evaluation
"Be thou diligent to know the state of thy flocks, and look well to thy herds." Proverbs 27:23

It now becomes necessary to examine each of our children in light of the Bible principles explained in this chapter. Here are the two questions we must ask and then answer with complete candor:

Has my child's spirit been born again?

And if so, is my child developing a spiritual strength that supersedes his physical and intellectual development?

Step Two - Pointed Prayer
"...ye have not, because ye ask not." James 4:4b

Time spent in honest evaluation of ourselves or our children should always be followed by a season of prayer. We need God's help and grace in the rearing of our children. Make the dream a daily prayer request. Pray for your children by name and ask God to give each of them spiritual strength. Then ask for the grace to be the right example to them and the wisdom to help teach them this important, Christian character trait.

Step Three - Parental Modeling
"My son, give me thine heart, and let thine eyes observe my ways." Proverbs 23:26

Remember, most important character traits are as much caught as taught. Our attitude and our actions will be replicated. This to me is the most humbling and fearful aspect of child rearing. It keeps me praying and motivates me to do right. I want to be the right example to my children.

Ask yourself these questions and answer them honestly: Which of the three types of mankind examined previously in this chapter best reflects my order of priorities and personal strengths -- the spiritual man, the athlete/beauty queen, or the intellectual/philosopher? When it comes to strength, which of my three main parts (spirit, soul or body) rule the other two? Which of the three do I spend the most time feeding and exercising? Do my children have a father and mother who are spiritually strong?

Step Four - Patient Instruction
"My son, hear the instruction of thy father, and forsake not the law of thy mother." Proverbs 1:8

It is up to us to help our children develop spiritual strength. It is vital that we use the tool of verbal instruction to instill in them the proper priorities in life.

1.   Teach them to have the proper heroes.

Go into your child's room. Look at the posters on the walls. Who are your children's heroes? Is your daughter impressed with women who possess outward beauty yet are devoid of inward virtue? Do her role models most resemble the strange woman of Proverbs chapter seven or the virtuous woman of Proverbs chapter thirty-one? Does your son look up to sports stars or spiritual leaders?

2.   Teach them to have the proper priorities.

Activities that increase spiritual strength should always take top priority. Bible reading is as vital as breakfast. Time on their knees praying is as important as time in front of the mirror primping. Personal holiness is as important as proper personal hygiene. A clean heart is as important as clean hands.

Do we spend hours teaching them to pass a ball, but never have taught them to pass out a Gospel tract? Do we run them to ball practice three times a week but cannot take them to the nursing home service once a month? Do we brag to others more about our children's aca-

31

demic achievements or their Christian character?

3. Teach them to have the proper balance.

I want you to understand that it is important that our children develop in all three areas as they grow to maturity. I am not against a child being involved in athletics or excelling academically. But we must always remember that Christ's example teaches us that spiritual development should supersede all else.

Step Five - Practical Training
"Train up a child in the way he should go; and when he is old, he will not depart from it." Proverbs 22:6

The Bible identifies three spiritual vitamins that contribute greatly to the development of spiritual strength.

1. We can help our children develop strength of spirit by teaching them to pray.

"Watch and pray, that ye enter not into temptation: the spirit indeed is willing, but the flesh is weak." Matthew 26:41

"But they that wait upon the LORD shall renew their strength; they shall mount up with wings as eagles; they shall run, and not be weary; and they shall walk, and not faint." Isaiah 40:31

Our spirit gains strength when it spends time before the throne of grace. Mothers, pray with your children. Dads, pray with your sons and daughters. Teach them by example to take their concerns and petitions to the Lord.

2. Our child's spirit is strengthened by the consumption of spiritual food.

"For the flesh lusteth against the Spirit, and the Spirit against the flesh: and these are contrary the one to the other: so that ye cannot do the things that ye would." Gal 5:17

My father was fond of an illustration that he used often in his early days of preaching. The story is told of an American Indian chief who was led to Christ by a missionary. Several weeks later, the missionary came to visit the chief and asked how his new Christian life was progressing.

"I feel like two dogs now live inside me. A black one and a white one. And they are always fighting."

"Who wins?" the missionary ventured.

"The one I feed the most, " replied the chief.

We are spiritually weak because we fail to gather our manna each morning from God's precious Word. We are spiritually weak because we spend so much time feeding the flesh with Hollywood movies, TV sitcoms, worldly pleasures and entertainment. Spirituality then must become an act, an outward facade. We build this wall tall and wide and garnish it with spiritual trappings, hoping no one will notice that behind it, our big, strong, black dog is devouring the little white one.

3. Our child's spirit is strengthened through the singing of psalms, hymns, and spiritual songs.

"And be not drunk with wine, wherein is excess; but be filled with the Spirit; Speaking to yourselves in psalms and hymns and spiritual songs, singing and making melody in your heart to the Lord;" Ephesians 5:18-19

"Let the word of Christ dwell in you richly in all wisdom; teaching and admonishing one another in psalms and hymns and spiritual songs, singing with grace in your hearts to the Lord." Colossians 3:16

Music is a powerful tool in molding and strengthening our children. If a song is "spiritual", then the words, the rhythm, and the beat of that song will all minister to a child's reborn spirit. Guard diligently against the influence of the wrong types of music finding their way into your child's life. Hard rock, soft rock, country, rap, and other "alternative" types of music are all designed to excite the flesh or promote destructive emotions and attitudes. Don't try to compromise with the world in their attempt to marry Christian words to a worldly, sensual beat.

A teenager came up to me once and challenged me on my stand against Christian rock and contemporary Christian music.

"I have taken some of my lost friends to Christian rock concerts and a few of them got saved at these concerts," she told me. "Young people are attracted to the rock and roll beat. If the musicians use these opportunities to present the Gospel, I don't see how you can criticize them."

I congratulated her for having a concern for her lost friends. I then offered a few more suggestions that might help her in her efforts to see more of them saved.

"Have you ever considered starting a Christian brewery? Young people seem to be attracted to beer. You could use the brand name, "Romans Road Suds." On the beer can could be printed the plan of salvation. Or maybe, "John 3:16 cigarettes." Every pack would have this evangelistic verse printed clearly on the back. Or maybe, a magazine called "Salvation Illustrated." I know that young men are attracted to things of the flesh. We could publish a provocative swim-suit edition, with each of the sensual women pictured holding verses printed on poster board."

"But that would be blasphemous!" she interrupted.

Exactly! I read to her Galatians 5:17 and explained that the flesh and Spirit of God are, *"contrary the one to the other: so that ye cannot do the things ye would."* The idea that we can excite the flesh then minister to the spirit is ridiculous. I cannot judge whether her friends were saved or not, but I do not believe that young people are capable of making spiritual decisions at the end of an evening spent provoking and exciting carnal emotions and fleshly desires.

The point is, create in your home an environment where your children's spirits are strengthened through good Christian music. Buy them Christian music and encourage them to play it in their rooms each morning as they get ready for the day. Have it playing in the dining room as they eat their breakfast. Good, Christ-honoring music is like taking spiritual vitamins!

Step Six - Praise and Reward
"The wicked worketh a deceitful work: but to him that soweth righteousness shall be a sure reward." Proverbs 11:18

Why do we offer our children incentives for bringing home good grades on their report cards, but never reward them for faithfully having personal devotions? Why do we award trophies for athletic achievements but never give out trophies for consistent Christian char-acter? Why do we compliment children on their outward beauty such as "She is so cute!" or "He is such a handsome young man!" but never say things like, "She is so faithful!" or "He has such a love for the Lord!"?

Listen carefully to what your children say. Verbally correct them if you hear them parroting the world's estimation of greatness. Refuse to let them become enamored with the development of their body or their mind at the expense of their spiritual development. The world will bombard them with its humanistic philosophies. We must be diligent to correct wrong thinking!

Part Two
Chapter 2

Godly Wisdom

"And the child grew, and waxed strong in spirit, filled with wisdom: and the grace of God was upon him." Luke 2:40

In my book, *The Teenage Years of Jesus Christ*, I tell teenagers that the number one priority of their teenage years is the pursuit of wisdom. From the age of twelve and upward, the Bible tells us, Jesus "increased in wisdom" (Luke 2:52). By definition, He added to what was already there. The reason it was already there was that during His previous twelve formative years, His parents saw to it that He was "filled with wisdom".

How do we rear wise children? What do we do to see to it that by the age of twelve, a child is filled with as much wisdom as his maturity level will allow? Again, let's put to good use our Biblical Parental Ladder!

Step One: Proper Evaluation
"Be thou diligent to know the state of thy flocks, and look well to thy herds." Proverbs 27:23

First of all we have to understand what we receive when God

blesses us with a baby. Instead of the doctor saying to the new parents, "Congratulations! It's a boy." or "Congratulations! It's a girl", perhaps the honest doctor should say, "Congratulations! It's a sinner!" Every newborn possesses two prominent characteristics in relationship to wisdom.

1. *Every child is born simple.*

Wisdom is not already instilled in them. They come untaught and untrained. It is up to his parents to replace a child's simplicity with Godly wisdom.

2. *Every child is born foolish.*

They have a built-in sin nature. You will not have to teach them to misbehave, they already know how. You will not have to train them to disobey, they will be prone to do that from the beginning. *"Foolishness is bound in the heart of a child...."* Proverbs 22:15. Foolishness comes as part of the original package.

It is important to understand what we are up against. If you do not have a plan, a ladder, to get your children from where they are to where they ought to be, chances are they will grow up simple and foolish. *"...a child left to himself bringeth his mother to shame."* Proverbs 29:15

3. *Our job as parents is to eliminate our children's simplicity and foolishness and to replace these with knowledge, understanding and wisdom.*

This chapter will give you the tools needed to do so!

The Simple, the Foolish and the Wise

Before we look at the Biblical steps necessary to replace simplicity with wisdom and to drive out foolishness, let's properly define all three of these terms.

1. *A simple child is ignorant of Bible commands and principles.*

He has never been taught so he just doesn't know. There are many children in America who are never taken to church, never sit under a Sunday School lesson. and never have been taught the Ten Commandments. Because of their simplicity, they are prone to foolish behavior. Their ignorance fuels their sin nature.

2. A foolish child, when taught Bible commands and principles, may choose to ignore them or directly disobey them.

Sometimes our children will exercise their free will in choosing to disregard the careful teaching and training of the parents. When a child does this, he commits an act of foolishness. If foolishness is not removed by carefully following the Scriptural instruction, it may dominate the child throughout his life.

3. A wise child hears, learns and obeys the commands and principles of God's Word.

He does this, not because it comes naturally, but because he has developed a heart for God, he has been taught and trained to do so, and scripturally corrected when he fails to do so.

Remember, every child is born simple with a built-in tendency toward foolishness. You must honestly evaluate your children. How do they respond when they receive a direct command? First, make sure they are old enough to understand what you are asking of them. Never punish a child for being simple. Simplicity is overcome by teaching and training, not correction.

A simple child has not been properly taught or trained. A foolish child has received the proper teaching and training, but refuses to obey, or delays obeying when possible. A wise child will cheerfully and willingly follow your instructions. How do we replace simplicity with wisdom? How do we help them overcome the pull toward disobedience?

Step Two - Pointed Prayer
"If any of you lack wisdom, let him ask of God,
that giveth to all men liberally, and upbraideth not; and it shall be
given him." James 1:5

Proper evaluation should always be followed by pointed prayer. The most daunting task you will face as a parent is to instill Godly wisdom into your children. God promises to give wisdom in answer to prayer! Acknowledge to God that you lack the wisdom to rear Godly children. Pray for wisdom—for yourself, and for your children.

Step Three - Parental Modeling
"My son, give me thine heart, and let thine eyes
observe my ways." Proverbs 23:26

Before we go any further, we must once again take stock of ourselves. The example we set before our children is powerful. Are we wise? Remember, God defines simplicity, foolishness and wisdom in relation to our ability and willingness to obey the principles set out in His Holy Word.

Are you simple concerning the Scriptures? Do you have an understanding of the truths of God's Word? If not, you can begin now to increase your understanding of the Scriptures by three Scriptural exercises:

1. Personal Study. In my book, *The Teenage Years of Jesus Christ*, I give simple instruction on how to study the Bible. Every Christian should not only read the Bible each day, but study the Bible each day.

2. Public Preaching. God has chosen to use the "foolishness of preaching" (foolish to the lost world, not to the born-again believer) to educate Christians concerning the Scriptures. Don't miss a church service! You can learn so much by faithfully sitting under a godly pastor. Your pastor loves you and wants to help you grow spiritually. Attend church as an expectant student, anxious and eager to learn what God wants to teach you through the messages delivered.

3. Private Counsel. The wise student goes beyond personal study and public preaching, and seeks out private counsel. If you have questions concerning the Bible, set up an appointment with your pastor and allow him to answer your questions and help you grow in your knowledge of the Scriptures.

As you learn Biblical truth, be anxious and willing to apply these truths to your life! Remember, foolishness is displayed when we understand clear instruction, but refuse to apply it to our lives and let it transform us into the image of Jesus Christ.

Step Four - Patient Instruction
"My son, hear the instruction of thy father, and forsake not the law of

thy mother." Proverbs 1:8

Simplicity is removed and wisdom is acquired by verbal instruction.

"...The Lord said unto me, Gather the people together, and I will make them hear my words, that they may learn to fear me all the days that they shall live upon the earth, and that they may teach their children." Deuteronomy 4:10

"And these words, which I command thee this day, shall be in thine heart: and thou shalt teach them diligently unto thy children..." Deuteronomy 6:6-7

"My son, hear the instruction of thy father, and forsake not the law of thy mother." Proverbs 1:8

"Receive my instruction, and not silver; and knowledge rather than choice gold." Proverbs 8:10

"Hear instruction, and be wise, and refuse it not." Proverbs 8:33

"Whoso loveth instruction loveth knowledge: but he that hateth reproof is brutish." Proverbs 12:1

"A fool despiseth his father's instruction..." Proverbs 15:5

"Apply thine heart unto instruction, and thine ears to the words of knowledge." Proverbs 23:12

Two things stand in the way of our children becoming wise: simplicity and foolishness. First, let's tackle the removal of simplicity. Simplicity is eliminated through verbal instruction. It is the parents' responsibility to teach their children the "words of knowledge". Verbal instruction provides wisdom on two levels.

1. Verbal instruction provides the child with knowledge.

The knowledge given to the child gives him the foundation to develop wisdom. Knowledge makes up the building blocks of wisdom and is provided to them through verbal instruction.

2. Verbal instruction reveals the child's attitude toward instruction.

The foolishness that is built into them will find its way to the surface rather quickly. Have you ever tried to instruct a toddler on how to do something, and have him respond in one of the following ways?

"I know. I know already!"

"I want to do it myself."

"No, I want to do it my way."

"I don't like you telling me how to do it!"

Or perhaps they get angry when you try to give them instruction. Or worse, just ignore you and continue on doing it their way. CAREFUL! If you ignore these words and actions, then you are allowing foolishness to strengthen its hold on your child. A child's attitude toward instruction reveals volumes about him!

In the previous verses, we learn that a wise person views instruction as something valuable; more valuable than silver or gold. He loves instruction and applies his heart to receive it. On the contrary, a "brutish man" hates reproof and a fool "despiseth his father's instruction."

Verbal instruction prevents a child from remaining simple, but it does not make him choose to be wise. Remember, simplicity is the result of having never been taught. Instruction forces the child to make a choice. What will he do with the instruction he receives? A wise child embraces and applies instruction, but a foolish child despises to obey it. God's Word teaches us that foolishness can be removed and we will cover that. But first, let's finish removing his simplicity.

Step Five - Practical Training
"Train up a child in the way he should go; and when he is old, he will not depart from it." Proverbs 22:6

Simplicity is removed and wisdom is acquired by practical training. Verbal instruction is important, but it is only the first step in removing simplicity. Practical training must accompany verbal instruction. Let me illustrate.

I began to give each of our daughters a small weekly allowance. This money was given as a reward for their diligence in fulfilling their weekly chores. This gave my wife and I an opportunity to teach them wisdom in the handling of money. From this allowance they were trained to tithe and to give to missions. Each had a savings account, and each was trained to place a little aside weekly for the future. Even what they were allowed to keep and spend gave us opportunity to train into them wise spending habits. We at times allowed them to make less than wise choices and then to learn from the consequences of those choices.

There is nothing like hands-on training. Classroom instruction has its place, but we must *do* to learn.

Step Six - Praise and Reward
"The wicked worketh a deceitful work: but to him that soweth righteousness shall be a sure reward." Proverbs 11:18

The combination of verbal instruction, practical training, and praise and reward produces young people who are confident and capable of performing an assigned task. Don't fail to praise them as they learn. Be patient -- remember back to when you were a child. It takes time to learn. But as you teach and train, be aware of your children's attitude toward instruction.

Step Seven - Purposeful Correction
"The rod and reproof give wisdom, but a child left to himself bringeth his mother to shame." Proverbs 29:15

Verbal instruction and practical training eliminate simplicity, but they do not guarantee that the child will be wise. What they do is force him to make a choice. When he chooses to ignore or disobey parental instruction, he has chosen to be foolish. *"A fool despiseth his father's instruction..." (Proverbs 15:5)* When our children display foolish tendencies, we must not ignore them, but rather deal with them immediately so that their attitude toward instruction is corrected.

Foolishness is driven out and wisdom is acquired by Biblical correction.

Many actions and attitudes are clearly labeled in the Bible as foolishness. But at the core, foolishness is simply disobedience or disdain toward a clear Biblical principle or command. If a child has been taught and trained to do right and simply refuses to do so, he is being foolish.

Foolishness is removed by the two "R's" of correction: reproof and the rod.

"The rod and reproof giveth wisdom: but a child left to himself bringeth his mother to shame." Proverbs 29:15

1. Always start with verbal reproof.

This is how we would wish for God to deal with us. If I am doing something that displeases the Lord, He always seems to bring it to my attention through the instrument of His Word. Either in my personal devotions or through public preaching, He says to me, "Hey, what you are doing is wrong and you know it. Now stop it." God does not watch me, hoping I will mess up so He can nail me. Spanking should never be the first option. Always correct first with reproof. Reprove, remind and retrain. Then expect the child's action and attitude to change. Don't be one of those parents who is always saying, "If you do that one more time..." Take a moment to reprove, remind and retrain. Then warn the child that if there is not an immediate change in actions and attitudes, you will move on to the second "R".

2. If verbal reproof is ignored, administer corporal punishment.

By corporal punishment, I mean administer a spanking.

I am a Bible-believing, fundamental preacher. I also am a Bible-believing, fundamental parent. I happen to believe that God knows more about child rearing than the afternoon TV talk show hosts who condemn proper, Scriptural, corporal punishment as child abuse. Considering the fact that most of these Hollywood hosts -- who consider themselves "child experts" -- are actively involved in adultery, fornication and/or homosexuality, it should not surprise us that they do not believe what the Bible says about child rearing.

On the other hand, I also believe that we should strictly follow the Bible principles that guide us in this matter. We should have a clear Bible reason for administering a spanking. We should also administer it properly and Biblically. If we do not, a spanking will not eliminate foolishness nor give wisdom.

When Should I Use Corporal Punishment?

1. The purpose for spanking a child is to drive out foolishness, not eliminate simplicity.

"Foolishness is bound in the heart of a child; but the rod of correction shall drive it far from him." Proverbs 22:15

What is foolishness? An act of foolishness is committed when a child -- who has been taught and trained to do right -- knowingly chooses to do just the opposite. If a child does something wrong and it is a result of our lack of teaching or training, then they did so out of simplicity. In that case, you may want to spank yourself, but don't spank your child! Instead, correct the behavior through teaching and training.

However if your child, as an act of defiance, exhibits behavior opposite of what he knows is right, then he has committed an act of foolishness. At this point, reprove him. Stop everything you are doing and get his attention. Then firmly rebuke him. Do not yell at him or raise your voice. Use this occasion to remind him of what he has been taught and trained to do. Then, if the behavior persists, or the offence is soon repeated, spank the child.

2. A spanking should be a spiritual lesson that allows the child to understand the character of God.

"My son, despise not the chastening of the LORD; neither be weary of his correction: For whom the LORD loveth he correcteth; even as a father the son in whom he delighteth." Proverbs 3:11-12

The parent who ignores or excuses acts of foolishness in their children instills within their children a warped view of Almighty God. God does not take pleasure in fools. If your children are saved, God ultimately is their Father. Children tend to form their impressions of God based upon the actions -- or inaction -- of their earthly parents. A child who does not fear to do wrong in your presence will grow up not fearing to do wrong in God's presence.

3. A spanking should always be motivated by love.

"For whom the LORD loveth he correcteth;" Proverbs 3:12

"He that spareth his rod hateth his son: but he that loveth him chasteneth him betimes." Proverbs 13:24

Years ago, I watched a liberal, so called child-rearing "expert" being interviewed on TV. The subject of spanking a child came up and she got so incensed at the notion that she stopped talking to the man interviewing her, looked directly into the camera, pointed her finger into my living room, and made this statement:

"Don't you dare claim to love your children, then turn them over your knee and spank them. You don't love your children if you spank them!"

Funny. God says just the opposite. God looks right down from Heaven and points His finger in our faces and says, "If you spare the rod you hate your children. If you love them, you will chasten them early."

Now, who are you going to believe?

The motivation for spanking a child is love. A wise parent who studies God's Word knows that it teaches that there is a lifetime of consequences awaiting the fool. If a child does not have removed "far from him" the tendency to ignore, despise and disobey clear Biblical instructions he will live a lifetime full of regrets, disappointments, and heartaches.

What are the consequences of foolishness? Here are just a few:

- **Destruction** — *"For the turning away of the simple shall slay them, and the prosperity of fools shall destroy them."* Proverbs 1:32
- **Shame** — *"The wise shall inherit glory: but shame shall be the promotion of fools."* Proverbs 3:35
- **Correction**—*"He goeth after her straightway, as an ox goeth to the slaughter, or as a fool to the correction of the stocks;"* Prov. 7:22
- **Death** —*"The lips of the righteous feed many: but fools die for want of wisdom."* Proverbs 10:21
- **Judgment** —*"Judgments are prepared for scorners, and stripes for the back of fools."* Proverbs 19:29
- **Punishment** — *"A whip for the horse, a bridle for the ass, and a rod for the fool's back."* Proverbs 26:3

I love my children too much to want that kind of a life for them. I want them to enjoy the blessings that come from a life lived in obedience to God and His Word. That will not happen if I do not do my duty as a parent in helping them to become wise.

4. Spanking should be done early.

"... he that loveth him chasteneth him betimes." Proverbs 13:24

As mentioned above, spanking should be done early or "betimes". In the back of the *Strong's Exhaustive Concordance* of the Bible is a Hebrew and Aramaic Dictionary. The word *betimes* is derived from the word *dawn*. It goes on to explain the meaning of the word as follows: *to be early at any task with the implication of earnestness; to search for with painstaking.* We have been taught by God that foolishness "is bound" in a child's heart. As parents, we ought to painstakingly watch for it. It will be displayed early and it should be corrected early. As soon as a toddler is taught what the word "no" means, he will test you. I know this because he has a sin nature. To understand that you said "no" and to look at you and do what he has been instructed not to do, is an act of foolishness. If you ignore it, you reinforce it. Remember: teach, train, rebuke, and if necessary, spank.

For every ounce of foolishness you remove from your child as a toddler, you eliminate a ton of rebellion that you will not have to deal with when he becomes a teenager.

5. A spanking, properly administered, will never threaten the child's health or life.

"Withhold not correction from the child: for if thou beatest him with the rod, he shall not die." Proverbs 23:13

Society has used the word "beat" so often in association with child or spousal abuse that we have a tendency to recoil when we see it. (i.e.: "He beats his wife" or "He beats his children.") I think Satan has worked very hard to cause this word to be linked with a criminal act because he knows it is a Bible word. However, again using the Hebrew dictionary in the back of our *Strong's Concordance*, we see that the word *beat* means "to strike, lightly or severely, literally or figuratively". That leaves a broad area for interpretation so we must study the word in the context of its usage.

Never should a child be struck in a manner that would cause injury or death. God has created an area on their behind (buttocks) that has plenty of extra fat and flesh, where you can strike a child lightly enough not to cause any injury while at the same time causing the child immense physical discomfort.

6. Tears of repentance are the desired effect of spanking.

This crying should be tears of remorse, not tears of anger and defiance.

"Chasten thy son while there is hope, and let not thy soul spare for his crying." Proverbs 19:18

A child should receive a spanking even if he begins to cry before it is administered. Foolishness is driven from a child by the use of corporal punishment, not by the tears of self-pity in anticipation of the spanking.

7. A child's tears should be as much from your disappointment as from your spanking.

What I am about to say is the most important truth concerning the use of corporal punishment that we can learn. Spankings should hurt their heart as much as their rear-ends.

"My son, give me thine heart..." Proverbs 23:26

If you have not built a close, loving, meaningful relationship with your child, spanking them will not bring about the desired affect. Love your children. Spend time with them. Applaud every time they do right. Praise them. Hold them, kiss them, cuddle them.

Then, if it is necessary, because of an act of foolishness, spank them. Spank them because it is the right and Biblical thing to do. The truth is, if you have the right relationship with your children, the broken fellowship and parental disappointment that their actions have created will bring more godly sorrow to their heart than anything else.

"My son if thine heart be wise, my heart shall rejoice, even mine." Proverbs 23:15

Every parent reading this has been bombarded with the idea that spanking a child is wrong. Magazine articles, newspaper stories, TV experts, celebrities and liberal child psychologists, - even unsaved (and sometimes saved!?!) family members have condemned it. There comes a time when we have to decide if we believe God or man. What is at stake is our child's earthly future and often, eternal destination.

"Withhold not correction from the child: for if thou beatest him with the rod, he shall not die. Thou shalt beat him with the rod, and shalt deliver his soul from hell." Proverbs 23:13-14

Primarily, wisdom is acquired by observation.

"My son, give me thine heart, and let thine eyes observe my ways." Proverbs 23:26

As important as verbal instruction, practical training, and Biblical correction may be, the old adage, "Wisdom is as much caught as taught" points us back to the man in the mirror. Wisdom must be modeled before our children on a daily basis. Having children will open your eyes more to your own shortcomings than any other thing I know. As a parent, strive to make the attainment of wisdom one of your principal goals. Get wisdom with all thy getting! Because ultimately, wise parents raise wise children.

Part Two
Chapter 3

Divine Graciousness

*"And the child grew, and waxed strong in spirit, filled with wisdom: and **the grace of God was upon him**." Luke 2:40*

*"And the Word was made flesh, and dwelt among us (and we beheld his glory, the glory as of the only begotten of the Father,) **full of grace and truth**." John 1:14*

*"And of his fulness have all we received, and **grace for grace**. For the law was given by Moses, but **grace and truth came by Jesus Christ**." John 1:16-17*

*"The **grace of our Lord Jesus Christ** be with you all. Amen." Romans 16:24*

I think the greatest definition of grace is a simple and oft repeated one. Grace is "unmerited favor". When the word grace is found in the Bible, it can either stand for the *act of grace* or the *attribute of graciousness*. We know that Jesus did not need to be shown grace - unmerited favor - because He was the sinless, perfect Son of God. In Luke 2:40, the phrase connecting grace and the Christ child could accurately be stated, "...and the graciousness of God was upon him." The third great attribute of Jesus as a child was *graciousness*.

In the late Dr. Jack Hyles' book, *Fundamentalism in My Lifetime*, he lists three common attributes of the greatest Christian men he had known during his lifetime.

1. *Each man was a man of great prayer.*
2. *Each man could point back to a moment where they believed that they were filled with the Holy Spirit for the first time.*
3. *Each man was a gracious man.*

Of all the attributes of greatness that could have been mentioned, I think it noteworthy that graciousness made the top three. The attribute of graciousness merits our attention.

I had the undeserved privilege of preaching with my father, Pastor Robert Ross, and Dr. Lee Roberson in a preaching conference in Cahokia, Illinois during the summer of 1994. My father preached a message entitled *The Symphony*, right before Dr. Roberson preached. When Dr. Roberson stood to preach, he called my name and asked me to stand. In front of the entire conference, he commissioned me to see to it that my father's message was put in booklet form. He said he would pay to see it done because, in his words, "every church member in America needs to hear that message."

Twice during that conference I preached right before Dr. Roberson. I preached short, Biblical messages and then got out of the way! The people hadn't come to hear me, they had come to hear Dr. Roberson. Here is an excerpt from a letter I received from him a week later:

June 3, 1994
Dear Brother Ross,
I just finished a letter to your father. I am rejoicing in his ministry in the meeting in Cahokia. I am writing you to thank you for the sermon which you gave to us! Every message was excellent, both in outline and in illustration. My wife and I agree that you are one of the finest young preachers we have heard in a long time....

Sincerely,
Lee Roberson

I cherish the letter to this day, and share it with you not because I was deserving of his time or his compliments. I share it with you to illustrate a simple truth: *the greater the man, the greater his graciousness!* At the time, my father and I both pastored small churches in rural towns. Seldom did either of us preach away from our own pulpits, but you would have thought that Dr. Roberson believed the people had come to hear us instead of him! What an impact it made on me as a young preacher. I vowed to copy his graciousness in my interaction with people.

If our children are going to be great in the eyes of the Lord, we need to work diligently to instill in them the attribute of graciousness.

Step One: Proper Evaluation

"Be thou diligent to know the state of thy flocks, and look well to thy herds." Proverbs 27:23

Many children today are anything but gracious. They are interested only in themselves and are usually fiercely jealous if a sibling or friend receives more attention or praise. This outlook on life is completely anti-Bible. It is the antithesis of Christ-likeness, and I am afraid to say that it is not restricted to just children. Immaturity in Christians today can be traced back to a lack of teaching and training in this area of graciousness.

Listen to your children. Listen to them as they interact with each other and with other children at church. Could it be said that they are blessed with a divine graciousness? Is it evident that the graciousness of God is upon them?

Step Two - Pointed Prayer
"...ye have not, because ye ask not." James 4:4b

By now, we are developing a daily prayer list for our children. How important it is that we pray! We need to call out the names of our children before the throne of grace. Pray daily that each child would develop strength of spirit. Pray that each would increase in wisdom, and pray that each would be anointed with a divine graciousness.

Step Three - Parental Modeling
"My son, give me thine heart, and let thine eyes observe my ways." Proverbs 23:26

Model graciousness before your children in your interaction with others. Return good for evil. Extend kindness to those who have done nothing to deserve it. Pray for those who have decided to be your enemies and invest in those who don't seem to care or appreciate it. After all, that is what Christ did for us.

Your children need to see you practicing pure religion.

"Pure religion and undefiled before God and the Father is this, To visit the fatherless and widows in their affliction, and to keep themselves unspotted from the world." James 1:27

Step Four - Patient Instruction
"My son, hear the instruction of thy father, and forsake not the law of

How can we make graciousness, this characteristic of greatness, a standard in our children's outlook and conduct?

1. Make your children well acquainted with the definition of grace.

Grace is God's favor and blessings bestowed upon an undeserving people. He does this because of what He is, not because of what we are. One man said, "*Mercy* is God not giving us what we really deserve and *grace* is God giving us what we don't deserve."

I have developed a habit of late. Whenever I read the Bible and come across the word grace, I say "unmerited favor". Whenever I join in the congregational singing in our church, and the song we are singing contains the word grace, as I sing the word I think, "unmerited favor."

"Amazing 'unmerited favor' how sweet the sound, that saved a wretch like me..."

God owed me nothing! What makes grace amazing, is the fact that it is favor shown even though we have done nothing to deserve it.

2. Teach your children that salvation is provided for us as an act of grace on the part of Almighty God.

There is always a level of arrogance connected with those who believe in a works-based salvation. In the following verses, notice how boasting is connected to those who believe they can in some fashion work their way to Heaven.

"Two men went up into the temple to pray; the one a Pharisee, and the other a publican. The Pharisee stood and prayed thus with himself, God, I thank thee, that I am not as other men are, extortioners, unjust, adulterers, or even as this publican. I fast twice in the week, I give alms of all I possess. And the publican, standing afar off, would not lift up so much as his eyes unto heaven, but smote his breast, saying, God be merciful to me a sinner." Luke 18:10-13

"For by grace are ye saved through faith; and that not of yourselves: it is the gift of God: not of works, lest any man should boast." Ephesians 2:8-9

A person who believes that their salvation is a result — in whole or in part — of their own good works tends to be arrogant. An understanding of grace produces graciousness. Did you notice the sickening level of arrogance displayed by the Pharisee in Christ's parable?

Did you see this arrogance contrasted by the humility of the publican? One was a braggart and the other was humbly gracious. The Pharisee boasted and bragged, even in his prayers. He was trusting in his good works and expected God to be pleased with him based on his own merits. The publican understood that if he was to be forgiven, it would be an act of grace on the behalf of Almighty God. Jesus proclaimed the publican *"justified rather than the other,"* and then warned all of us in verse 14, *"...for everyone that exalteth himself shall be abased; and he that humbleth himself shall be exalted."*

If we got what we deserved, we all would spend eternity in a devil's hell! There is not one thing we can do to earn our way to Heaven. A child who truly understands what it means to be saved by grace alone, will have a basis — a divine example to live up to — in this matter of extending grace to others.

Teach your children often this simple truth. "Anything and everything we are allowed to enjoy in this life is an act of grace. Any circumstance or situation that we are asked to face, short of hell, is an act of grace."

3. Encourage them to extend graciousness to others on the same level that it was extended to them by Jesus Christ.

Remember, an understanding of God's amazing grace will produce in our children amazing graciousness. *"And be ye kind one to another, tenderhearted, forgiving one another, even as God for Christ's sake hath forgiven you." Ephesians 4:32*

Step Five - Practical Training
"Train up a child in the way he should go; and when he is old, he will not depart from it." Proverbs 22:6

1. Train them to have a humble spirit.

Do not raise a braggart. Have them memorize this verse early and then insist that they live by it. *"Let another man praise thee, and not thine own mouth; a stranger, and not thine own lips." Proverbs 27:2*

Insist that they learn to speak with graciousness to others. Listen to their comments and conversations. Don't allow them to develop a "smart mouth". Teach them that words are powerful! A carefully worded, well thought-out compliment can lift up a person's spirit and encourage him to live for God. A calloused, thoughtless comment can break a person's spirit and ruin his day.

"Let your speech be alway with grace, seasoned with salt, that ye may know how ye ought to answer every man." Colossians 4:6

2. Train them to be gracious and to be constantly aware of the graciousness of God to them.

- Train them to offer sincere thankfulness at every meal, not some rushed memorized prayer (vain repetition).
- Train them to prefer others above themselves — that there is more joy in letting someone else go first than in going first.
- Train them to reach out to young people at church who are new or who tend to be left out.
- Train into them common courtesies and simple manners.
- Train them how to graciously address their elders.
- Train them to smile when greeting others.
- Train them to take the time for people.
- Train them to steer a conversation away from themselves and learn to genuinely show an interest in the other person and what is going on in his life.
- Train them to express gratitude. Teach them the power of a simple thank-you note.
- Teach them to look people in the eye when shaking their hand.
- Teach them to defend anyone who is unjustly attacked.
- Teach them to look for needs to fill.
- Teach them this simple, yet powerful question: "Is there anything I can do to help you?"
- Teach them to remember birthdays and anniversaries.
- Teach them to pray for others as they meet them throughout the day.
- Teach them to avoid flattery, but to compliment people often. (Flattery is the *payment* of a compliment in hopes of *earning interest*. A compliment is kindness shown with no motive other than to uplift and encourage another.)
- Teach them to deflect credit to others when they are complimented.
- Teach them to appreciate people for who they are, and to under-

stand that the world would be a pretty boring place if there were not a diversity of personalities.

- Teach them the power of a hug, a touch on the arm, or a pat on the back when speaking to someone of like gender.
- Teach them to take the time for children younger than themselves.
- Teach them to learn to laugh at themselves.
- Teach them that most people are insecure and need reassurance.
- Teach them to take the time to talk to widows.
- Have them work on a church bus route or in a church nursing home ministry (pure religion).
- Teach them to be gracious in victory as well as in defeat.
- Teach them to learn to enjoy the simple, free things. Teach them that a spring shower, a beautiful sunrise, a maple tree on fire with its fall color change, and the first downy blanket of snow, are all gifts sent to us from a gracious God.
- Teach them that every day is a gift; a gift to be opened and used selflessly. And each day brings with it another chance to give out gifts of graciousness to others.

Step Six - Praise and Reward
"The wicked worketh a deceitful work: but to him that soweth righteousness shall be a sure reward." Proverbs 11:18

Everyone responds to praise. When you observe your child being gracious to another, later -- privately -- hold them close and let them know how pleased you are. If they sacrifice something to help someone else, at some point in time reward them in a tangible way.

Step Seven - Purposeful Correction
"The rod and reproof give wisdom, but a child left to himself bringeth his mother to shame." Proverbs 29:15

Teach them that selfishness is a devilish and wicked sin. Self-ishness is the avowed enemy of graciousness. Do not tolerate selfish actions or selfish attitudes. Every day that is lived for self is a day that will burn up at the judgment seat of Christ. Correct selfishness — never let it go unchallenged.

Part Two
Chapter 4

Hunger for Knowledge

"And it came to pass, that after three days they found him (Jesus) in the temple, sitting in the midst of the doctors, both hearing them and asking them questions." Luke 2:46

I once saw an artist's rendition of the scene depicted in the above verse. It showed an adolescent Christ surrounded by the aged members of the Sanhedrin, looks of amazement on their faces as the child appears to be instructing them. The caption below the painting read, "The Christ-child teaches the doctors." However, an accurate reading of the Scripture reveals to us that Christ did not go to the temple that day to teach, but rather to learn. He came to hear, and when He wanted clarification, He asked them questions. Jesus engaged them such for three days. Have you ever asked yourself why?

The answer is simple. Jesus was hungry for knowledge.

There are some who believe that it was during this session that He satisfied Himself through the Old Testament prophecies that He was indeed the Messiah, the Promised One. I am not sure if I agree with this or not, but wouldn't it be interesting if God the Father allowed Jesus to discover His identity and purpose through a close examination of the Scriptures: that even the Living Word had to go to the Written Word for illumination and direction?

The picture I form in my mind as I read this story is of a twelve year old boy walking into the temple because He wanted some answers. When most twelve year old boys were playing childish games or strolling around enjoying the carnival-like atmosphere that permeated Jerusalem during the Passover Feast, something different was burning in the heart of the God-Child. He was hungry to learn, hungry for knowledge. Because of this He sought out those who would have the answers. He engaged these scholars, drawing from them knowledge that they had spent a lifetime gleaning.

Jesus wanted to know, wanted to learn.

Show me today where the young believers are who have an insatiable appetite for the truth. How can we as parents instill into our children a hunger for knowledge, a thirst for truth?

Using the Parental Ladder to Instill Within Our Children a Hunger for Knowledge

Step One: Proper Evaluation
"Be thou diligent to know the state of thy flocks, and look well to thy herds." Proverbs 27:23

Now it is time to compare our children to the Christ-child. Where is the hunger for knowledge, the burning desire to learn? As a Christian school administrator, I am often shocked at how hard some children work to avoid learning! There is a difference between finishing an assignment and learning the material. Skimming the material instead of reading the material, cramming instead of comprehending, and looking for shortcuts instead of mining for knowledge has become the norm.

How important is learning to your child? Is there a hunger to accumulate practical knowledge and Biblical principles? What is their attitude toward instruction and those who instruct? How much effort do they put into learning? Do they endure the Sunday School lesson or absorb it? During preaching, do they watch the pastor or watch the clock? What is their attitude toward school? Are they hungry?!?!

Read the following portion of Proverbs carefully!

"My son, if thou wilt receive my words, and hide my commandments with thee; so that thou incline thine ear unto wisdom, and apply thine heart to understanding; yea, if thou criest after knowledge and liftest up thy voice for understanding; if thou seekest her as silver and searchest for her as for hid treasures; then shalt thou understand the fear of the Lord, and find the knowledge of God. For the Lord giveth wisdom: out of his mouth cometh knowledge and understanding." Proverbs 2:1-5

We have allowed a generation to become mentally lazy! Television and video games have turned our children into dullards! We make excuses and invent imaginary "disorders" instead of teaching, training, and disciplining our children to think. We have allowed them to believe that the frivolous is important and the important is frivolous.

We must start with proper evaluation. The questions are simple ones. Do my children have a hunger to learn? Is knowledge important to them? If not, what can I do as a parent to change this?

Step Two - Pointed Prayer
"...ye have not, because ye ask not." James 4:4b

Involve God! There are three verses that I often quote to remind myself of the futility of our human effort if it is not divinely anointed and empowered. Notice that the first two verses precede an important child rearing verse.

"Except the Lord build the house, they labour in vain that build it: except the Lord keep the city, the watchman waketh but in vain. It is vain for you to rise up early, to sit up late, to eat the bread of sorrows: for so he giveth his beloved sleep. Lo, children are an heritage of the Lord: and the fruit of the womb is his reward." Psalms 127:1-3

We work hard, we keep watch, we start early, stay up late, worry and fret. We do everything but pray! Pray for your children, and high on the list of things to ask for them should be this simple request, "O Lord, put within my child a hunger for knowledge, a desire to know divine truth."

Step Three - Parental Modeling
"My son, give me thine heart, and let thine eyes observe my ways." Proverbs 23:26

I am fifty-one years old and am still a student. I will never graduate. Don't get me wrong, somewhere in my possession are my kindergarten diploma, my high school diploma and a college diploma, but I still believe that everyday God intends to teach me something new. I seldom pass up an opportunity to learn something new as long as it is something healthy and holy. I have an insatiable curiosity. I read. I study. I ask questions. I attend the school of life, and seek out spiritual and practical "doctors", to hear them and ask them questions.

If we are not interested in learning, our children will see little use for it. I have worked with teenagers for almost twenty-five years. Show me a teenager who listens casually to sermons, and seldom, if ever, responds to their truths and I will show you a parent who, more often than not, has the same attitude toward the instruction of God's Word. Show me a child who has a flippant attitude toward his school work, and somewhere in the shadows is a parent making comments like, "You'll never use that stuff anyway -- I don't even know why they teach it." We don't know what God will ask our children to do, and we would be wise to see to it that they are equipped properly in case He were to call them to an area of service where they will need what we have deemed "unimportant".

Step Four - Patient Instruction
"My son, hear the instruction of thy father, and forsake not the law of thy mother." Proverbs 1:8

If we are to instill into our children a hunger for knowledge, then we must instill within them three important attitudes. This is achieved by patient, repetitious, verbal instruction. Some things should be said over and over again, until they are engrained into our children's very being. Then, fifty years from now, they will be saying to their grandchildren, "You know what my dad used to say about that..." or "My mother used to always tell us..."

1. Teach them to fear the Lord.
"The fear of the Lord is the beginning of knowledge, but fools despise wisdom and instruction." Proverbs 1:7
We must rear our children to fear the Lord. This is the first step, the starting line in a life-long marathon that will, with each stride, bring them closer to the day when they will hold the trophies of knowledge, understanding and wisdom.

2. Magnify the importance of gathering knowledge.
Hold them accountable by asking them often, "What did you learn today?" What did you learn in your devotions? What did you learn in Sunday School? What did you learn from pastor's sermon? What did you learn in school today? To live a day without learning is to waste a day.

Teach them to take notes during sermons and lessons. Taking notes trains them to listen for important truths and key principles.

Knowledge can be gathered from everyone around them. My pastor for eight years, Dr. Jack Hyles, used to say, "Every person knows something that I do not know, therefore every man is my teacher."

3. Magnify the office of those who teach knowledge.

"My brethren, be not many masters, knowing that we shall receive the greater condemnation." James 3:1

Your pastor should be honored when he is spoken of in your home. Your children should be taught to respect anyone who holds the position of teacher -- whether it is a school teacher or a Sunday School teacher. They should address their teachers by the proper title. Your children should be taught to express their thankfulness regularly to anyone who takes time to share with them Godly, practical knowledge.

Pastors and teachers should be heroes to your children. If you spend time openly criticizing those whom God is using to teach your children divine knowledge, you not only sour your children's attitudes toward authority, you diminish their respect toward knowledge. Remember, you cannot teach selective disrespect. If you allow them to be disrespectful toward those who are trying to teach them, they will also have that same attitude toward you when you, as their parent, are trying to teach them.

Step Five - Practical Training
"Train up a child in the way he should go; and when he is old, he will not depart from it." Proverbs 22:6

1. Instill within them a love for reading.

One of the greatest gifts my parents gave me growing up was a steady supply of good books to read. My mother took us often to the public library. She allowed me to purchase books and build a modest library. I was a son of the woods. I loved to hunt and fish, and spent as much time as I could roaming and exploring the hills and "hollars" of Northern Clay County, Indiana. But seldom did I leave without a book tucked away somewhere on my person.

2. Treat their questions with great respect.

Notice that the twelve year old Christ not only listened as the doctors taught, but also asked them questions. Questions are one of the greatest tools a child has in gathering knowledge. You do not have to train a child to ask questions; remember the "Why?" phase? But if we are not careful, we can train them not to ask questions by our reaction to them. Because of this, we must treat their questions with great respect.

Many times our children's questions will seem silly to us. If we laugh or belittle them for their lack of knowledge, they will stop asking questions. Giving your children the impression that their questions are a bother will again cause them to stop asking. The Bible even teaches us the tone of voice that we use when answering a question or imparting knowledge can add to or diminish a child's ability to learn.

The wise in heart shall be called prudent: and the sweetness of the lips increaseth learning. Proverbs 16:21

A child's question gives us not only a great opportunity to increase their knowledge, but also an opportunity to develop their understanding. In the next chapter, we will show you how to answer your children's questions in such a way that they will not only receive the answer, but will have their reasoning skills developed.

Step Six - Praise and Reward
"The wicked worketh a deceitful work: but to him that soweth righteousness shall be a sure reward." Proverbs 11:18

Praise is such a powerful tool! What child does not bloom under the warm rays of his parents' approval? Proper behavior is cemented into place with parental praise. Fan your children's hunger for knowledge by congratulating them when they make any effort to learn. Learning can and should be fun! Work hard at making it so.

Step Seven - Purposeful Correction
"The rod and reproof give wisdom, but a child left to himself bringeth his mother to shame." Proverbs 29:15

In our chapter on instilling Godly wisdom, we found out that, although "foolishness is bound in the heart of a child", a combination of reproof and the rod can "drive it far from him."

How important are our children's attitudes toward instruction? How important is it that they set as a priority the gaining of Godly knowledge? Should a disdain for instruction and knowledge be tolerated or excused? Read the following verses and let the Word of God weigh in on the matter.

"The fear of the LORD is the beginning of knowledge: but fools despise wisdom and instruction." Proverbs 1:7

"Take fast hold of instruction; let her not go: keep her; for she is thy life." Proverbs 4:13

"Receive my instruction, and not silver; and knowledge rather than choice gold." Proverbs 8:10

"Hear instruction, and be wise, and refuse it not." Pr. 8:33

"Whoso loveth instruction loveth knowledge: but he that hateth reproof is brutish." Proverbs 12:1

"Poverty and shame shall be to him that refuseth instruction: but he that regardeth reproof shall be honoured." Proverbs 13:18

"He that refuseth instruction despiseth his own soul: but he that heareth reproof getteth understanding." Proverbs 15:32

Over and over again, God emphasizes the connection between wisdom and a hunger for knowledge. He also labels a disdain for instruction and knowledge as foolishness. As parents, we must see to it that our children are reared with a sacred attitude toward instruction, and with a genuine thirst to learn. To do otherwise is to rear fools.

Part Two
Chapter 5

Depth of Understanding

"And all that heard him were astonished at his understanding and answers." Luke 2:47

Let's again gear up our imaginations and let it take us back in time to the scene of the Christ child as He sits for three days in the temple, listening to the doctors and asking them questions. He is there because of His hunger for knowledge. But there is something that quickly becomes apparent to these learned, aged men, something that astonishes them. This child is no ordinary twelve year old. He not only listens; He understands. They begin to ask Him some questions to gauge the depth of His knowledge and understanding, and again they are amazed at His answers.

I taught high school in some capacity for ten years. I have been a Sunday School teacher for over thirty years. *There is a huge differ-*

ence between knowing what to do to get the correct answer and know-ing why you did what you did to get that correct answer!

Let me illustrate. A young person is finishing a page of algebra problems. I peek over his shoulder and he is getting them correct.

I ask him, "Do you know how to do these problems?"

"Sure! I just follow the example and do those same steps and so far I am getting them right."

Now for the important question. "Do you understand why they are coming out right?'

"Not really, but if I just keep mimicking what I see in the exam-ple, I'll be alright."

This student has knowledge, but no understanding. He is smart enough to memorize and repeat what is before him, but he does not un-derstand the "whys", or the mathematical principles, behind each step. Trust me, he will not be "alright".

Soon his hand will be raised and he will say, "I'm lost!". The reason is because all problems are not exactly like the example! It is not enough to have knowledge, you must also develop understanding.

Common Sense is Not-So-Common

Life is like algebra! It is always throwing you a curve ball. Not all problems can be solved with the same steps or the same formula. If a young person has spent his life gathering knowledge, but never really understands how to take that knowledge and put it in proper sequence to solve the unique problem before him, he will soon decide that maybe the knowledge is worthless. No. The knowledge is like a $1000 check -- valuable, but not spendable unless it is endorsed and turned into cash. Understanding is the ability to endorse and cash in on knowledge!

My grandfather's generation called this common sense. Com-mon sense is the ability to assimilate knowledge and put it into every-day use. It understands not just the "whats" but the "whys" behind the "whats".

A big challenge facing all parents in the rearing of their children during the first twelve years is teaching their children not just to mimic what they see you doing, but to understand why they are to do it. Most of our young people being reared in our fundamental churches are just mimicking the examples around them. They are OK so far, because the problems are not as hard as they soon will be. But if they do not develop their understanding, then they are not developing convictions. Bible convictions are a result of understanding Bible principles, of understanding the Bible reasons we do what we do -- or don't do what we don't do!

Step One: Proper Evaluation
"Be thou diligent to know the state of thy flocks, and look well to thy herds." Proverbs 27:23

Are you often astonished at the depth of your children's understanding? Have they developed the ability to listen and really hear your instructions? Do they have the ability to "isolate and concentrate" or are they easily distracted? Do they need to have step by step instructions, or are they developing the ability to think through a problem and find for themselves the proper solutions?

Step Two - Pointed Prayer
"...ye have not, because ye ask not." James 4:4b

"Lord, give my children understanding hearts. Please let them comprehend the depth of the truths from your Word. Give them insight. Please help the things I teach them not to simply be retained in their minds, but let it sink down into their very souls. Help them not just to memorize truth, but help them to embrace it and make it their very own."

Step Three - Parental Modeling
"My son, give me thine heart, and let thine eyes observe my ways." Proverbs 23:26

I want my children to learn to listen to me. I want them to be disciplined enough to focus on what I am saying and to learn to overcome distractions. I want them to believe that what I am telling them is important. I want them to learn to think things through -- to take the knowledge that I give them and search it to its depth.

I think my Heavenly Father wants the same for His children. My children need to see me giving to God the same attention and serious consideration to His Word that I ask them to give to my words.

Step Four - Patient Instruction
"My son, hear the instruction of thy father, and forsake not the law of thy mother." Proverbs 1:8

I did an eye-opening word study several years ago on the word "hear." I chased it from Genesis to Revelation. It was amazing how many times God has to ask us to stop and listen! All of us can improve in this area. Notice these verses in Proverbs that encourage this young man to open his ears and listen to what is being said.

"A wise man will hear, and will increase learning..." Prov. 1:5

"Hear, ye children, the instruction of a father, and attend to know understanding." Proverbs 4:1

"Hear me now therefore, O ye children, and depart not from the words of my mouth." Proverbs 5:7

"Hear; for I will speak of excellent things; and the opening of my lips shall be right things." Proverbs 8:6

"Hear instruction, and be wise, and refuse it not." Prov. 8:33

"Hear counsel, and receive instruction, that thou mayest be wise in thy latter end." Proverbs 19:20

"Bow down thine ear, and hear the words of the wise, and apply thine heart unto my knowledge." Proverbs 22:17

"Hear thou, my son, and be wise, and guide thine heart in the way." Proverbs 23:19

Did you notice how many times knowledge, understanding and wisdom are connected to hearing? If our children are not taught and trained to listen, they will never develop and grow as God would have them to.

How To Teach Your Children Mental Focus

Here are four good habits that need to be instilled into your children to help them develop the discipline of being a good listener.

1. Train them to look at the person who is talking to them.
Not only is this respectful, but it also helps them to stay focused on what is being said. No matter what they are busy doing, it is a sign of courtesy to stop what they are doing when someone begins to address them and to give that person their full attention.

2. Train them to develop physical and mental focus.

Everyone should have these three words printed and taped somewhere near their work station: *ISOLATE AND CONCENTRATE!* These words define focus. Focus is critical when learning to listen properly. We *isolate* when we ignore any physical distractions around us that are competing with the person who is speaking to us. We *concentrate* when we ignore any mental distractions -- other thoughts or ideas that might creep in—which keep us from hearing what the person in front of us is saying.

Isolate and concentrate! This is especially important in classroom situations or preaching services. Train your children to always look at the person who is up front speaking. If you are not looking at the speaker, chances are good you are not listening. Even if you are, it is again a sign of respect to look at the one addressing the crowd. That is part of giving them your "full attention".

Train your children to ignore disturbances in public services. This takes discipline. My father was insistent on this when we were small children being trained to sit in church. Someone behind us would cough or whisper or get up and slip out to the restroom and four little heads would turn to observe the distraction. I can sometimes still feel my father's large hand being placed on my head and turning it back toward the preacher. He explained to us children that we make a disturbance more of a disturbance by turning to look.

"You can never know who is in the service," he would tell us. "You causing a disturbance or accenting one by turning to look could distract someone's attention away from listening to the Gospel being preached. Don't allow yourself to be used as a tool by the devil to keep someone from being saved." I soon prided myself on the fact that I could concentrate on the preacher and ignore disturbances during the service, even though I noticed that many adults seemed to be unable to resist a peek over their shoulder. Now that I am a preacher myself, believe me, I understand what he was saying. Children -- and many adults -- in our congregations could use a little training in this area!

3. Eliminate from your children's vocabulary this response: "Huh?"

I was sitting in a college History Class that was being taught, when the professor stopped in the middle of a lecture, addressed a student, and then asked him a question. I don't remember the question but I remember the student's answer. He looked up at the professor and asked, "Huh?" That response was followed by this conversation -- a conversation that taught me an important lesson on listening.

Professor: *Did you say, "Huh?" Mr. *****.*

Student: *Yes sir, I'm sorry, I didn't hear your question.*

Professor: *Yes you did. Stop and think.*

Silence

Professor: *Now, what did I ask you?*

Student: *(Repeats the question word-perfect.)*

Professor: *See, I knew you heard the question. Now, why did you answer, "Huh?"*

Student: *I don't know.*

Professor: *Well, I will explain it to you. You answered "Huh?" because you are a lazy listener. You heard what I said, but it was easier for you to ask me to repeat it again than it was for you to focus and think about what I just said. "Huh?" is a bad habit. Focusing and listening to people when they speak to you is the mark of an intelligent man.*

The above exchange might seem a bit harsh to you, but we were college students. We were paying money to sit in that class and be taught. I learned a great lesson that day -- a lesson that I hope has made me a better listener.

4. Check to see if they are listening to you by occasionally asking them to repeat back to you what you said to them.

If they cannot, explain to them why they can't. Instruct them again on looking, focusing, and concentrating on the person who is speaking to them, and upon what they are saying. If they can repeat what you said, praise them! Bragging on their listening skills will make them try even harder to be a good listener.

Step Five - Practical Training
"Train up a child in the way he should go; and when he is old, he will not depart from it." Proverbs 22:6

A child must be trained to think. I cannot tell you the number of times as a boy -- after doing something that in hindsight was obviously going to end in disaster -- that one of my parents looked at me and with a perplexed tone of voice asked, "WHAT WERE YOU THINK-

ING!?!?"

My two brothers and I were raised in the country. We did not have a whole lot of material things growing up, so when we were young we had to invent our own amusements. I was recently given a card with a picture on the front of it that pretty much summed up our childhood. On the front of this card is a picture of two brothers. They are sitting in a child's red wagon that they had rebuilt into a "stage coach." The boys were both wearing tattered cowboy hats and plastic holsters holding their "six-shooters". One boy was in back and the other sat on a crate in front, getting ready to "drive" the stage coach. The wagon's handle was tied to a rope which in turn was looped around the neck of their pony, who was looking back at them with curiosity. The "driver" of the stage coach had in his hand a sling shot, at full draw, and was aiming it at the south-end of the north-bound pony!

I had to laugh. They were about to go for a ride! You might look at that picture and ask, "What were those boys thinking?" I can answer that. They weren't! Many times my dear mother had to grab one of us boys and rush us to the hospital because we failed to think through our plan to its obvious conclusion. Children seldom see the step beyond the immediate. Because of this, it is important that we train in them the ability to think through a problem.

Don't Answer All Your Children's Questions!!!

Over the years, I have been asked hundreds of questions a week. As a school administrator, teachers and staff members seek me out. When I was a high school teacher, I walked from desk to desk in response to the uplifted hands of dozens of students a day. As the father of three curious daughters, I was followed around and interrogated at home. I found a wonderful way to help all those who came to me with their questions.

I refused to answer them.

Before you conjure up images of a mute, antisocial, high brow let me assure you that I am nothing of the kind.

"Then why won't you answer the sincere questions of those who are reliant upon you for help and guidance?" you may ask.

Sorry, I can't just tell you the answer to that question. If I do, then you won't have to think.

The greatest mistake we as adults make is supplying answers to all of our children's questions. A much quoted proverb tells us, "If you give a man a fish, you feed him for a day. If you teach a man to fish, you feed him for a lifetime."

If you give a child an answer, you help him for a moment. If you teach a child to think, you help him for a lifetime."

Jesus made an amazing statement in Matthew 11:28-29. *"Come unto me, all ye that labour and are heavy laden and I will give you rest. Take my yoke upon you and learn of me."*

A child comes to you with a question. It is weighing upon his mind. It is a problem that he is mentally struggling to solve. It is a burden. Love does not lift it for him. Love does not take it from him.

Love offers a yoke.

A yoke is designed to combine the strength of two to pull a load that is too heavy for one alone. Your children will never develop the mental strength to solve their own problems if you simply give them the solutions. Join minds with them, help them get the wagon rolling, then back off and let them pull!

When a child asks you a question, he does so because he is thinking. The minute you give him the answer, he most likely will stop thinking. He doesn't have to think anymore. You gave it to him. However, if all you agree to do is help him toward the answer, he must continue to think until he discovers the answer for himself. Then he has not only learned an answer, but also discovered a road to an answer. A road he will use again and again in his life. He is developing what we call deductive reasoning.

You may be thinking, "Well, if I can't answer their questions, what can I do to help them?"

OK. Just this once I'm going to break my own rule and answer your question. Here are some tried and tested ways that you can use to help your child work his way to the answer he is seeking.

1. Ask a Question.

Not just any question, but a question designed to take them in the direction of the correct answer.

One of the seniors in our school stopped me after church. "Let me ask you a question. I finally found a car that I'm thinking of buying." He began to describe this car with zeal, obviously enamored with this sporty, but expensive roadster. I listened patiently, considering the future he was forgetting. I knew his plan was to attend college after graduation. I knew he would have to pay most of his own way. I knew he had been working and saving money for college for the past two summers, money that now was going to be spent on a nice, but extravagant vehicle.

"Well, what do you think? Should I get it?"

Oh, how tempting just to answer. To tell him what I think. Oh, how much wiser to engage him with questions. To help *him* to think.

"Sounds like a great car. Do you have a workable plan to pay for it and your first year of college?"

We talked for about five minutes. During that time I listened, asked four pointed questions to get him thinking, and left the door open for him to report back to me about his decision.

"Whatever you decide to buy, be sure to let me see it. I'm sure you'll make a wise choice."

A few weeks later, I followed him out to the parking lot to see his reliable and affordable selection. I asked him about the other car he had told me about. His answer was telling.

"I thought about it and decided to buy this instead. It cost a lot less and with college next year, I need to be careful."

He thought and he decided.

2. Narrow the Field.

When my daughters were younger, they played a game called "Seek and Find." It is a lot like "Hide And Seek," only instead of hiding from each other, they hid an object, such as a teddy bear, somewhere in the house. The one who was "it" then was allowed to leave her bedroom and search the entire house until the object was found or until she gave up. (I'm probably leaving out some important rules but you get the idea.) If she couldn't find the object and began to get frustrated, she appealed to the supreme judge of all childhood games, (that's my wife at our house) to make the other child "narrow the field." Upon her ruling, the child who had hidden the object specified the room that the object was in, but never revealed the exact location. Although it made it easier for the person looking, she must still, "seek and find."

It's OK to "narrow the field", but never give up the bear!

At school, a student and a teacher often have different goals. Most students want the answer so that they can finish the assignment. They want to be done. A good teacher also wants the student to finish, but he wants him to *learn* the material, not just complete it. And so begins the game of "can-I-get-the-teacher-to-tell-me-the-answer." In my class, no. But if you can convince me you are trying and I sense you are getting frustrated, I will narrow the field.

Billy raises his hand. "Mr. Ross, I've read this entire chapter twice and I can't find the answer to question six."

"Read the question out loud to me," I reply.

He complies. "In which state did Andrew Johnson serve as governor?"

"Now read to me just the main headings of the chapter on our former president."

"Early Life. Political and Public Activities. Administration as President. Later Years."

"Very good. In which of these sections do you feel the answer would most likely be found?"

"I'm not sure."

(Be very careful here. As a parent or a teacher, an answer that might be very obvious to us may totally escape a young person. Jesus said, *"Take my yoke upon you and learn of me; for I am meek and lowly in heart:"* A condescending attitude toward anyone's question will have one certain result: next time they won't ask.)

"I believe you will find your answer in the section headed, "Political and Public Activities." Since the question pertains to his time as governor, it would fall under the section on politics."

I've not given him *the* answer, but I've narrowed the field. I have not just given him the correct section but the reason why I chose that section. It is important that he work for the answer. As most parents know, a child only values what has cost him something!

3. Share a Story

Jesus was the Master at this. The Great Parable Teller seldom answered a question head on. He knew that He would only be with His disciples a few short years. He had to teach them to think spiritually on their own. Notice the question asked Him by a lawyer in Luke 10:25. *"Master, what shall I do to inherit eternal life?"*

Notice Christ's "answer." *"What is written in the law? How readest thou?"*

Two questions.

The lawyer answered, *"Thou shalt love the Lord thy God with all thy heart, and with all thy soul, and with all thy strength, and with all thy mind: and thy neighbor as thyself."*

Jesus agreed with his answer and instructed him to go and do it.

The lawyer then asked a qualifying question. *"And who is my neighbor?"*

The next six verses contain Christ's "answer", the parable of the Good Samaritan. This, of course, is the story of a man severely beaten and robbed and three men who had opportunity to help him— two who didn't, and one who did. At the end of the story, Jesus again asks a question.

"Which now of these three, thinkest thou, was neighbor unto him that fell among the thieves?"

Thinkest thou!

Two questions, a story, and a question. What a teacher!

The best answer to a child's question is often a story shared from the experience of your own life. A story from your childhood, from your own family, or even a story from the Bible. Tell the story, but don't draw the conclusion. Remember, our job is just to get the wagon rolling. They need to cross the finish line under their own power.

4. Supply a Resource.

"Can Satan make it rain?" I look into the eyes of a thin, under-sized seventh grade boy. He is serious. He's been thinking about this. He wants an answer.

"I don't know," I answer. No, this isn't a trick to get him to think. I really didn't know! Taking out a 3x5 card, I write out his question and put it back into my pocket.

"Give me a few days and I'll get back to you."

The next day I sat down at my desk, and there waiting for me is the card with his question printed on it. Glancing at the pile of work stacked in my tray, I sigh. Well, I did promise him. Pulling my concordance off the shelf, I look up the word "rain" and conduct a quick word study, jotting down a few things on the same card.

The next day he was waiting for me. Same curious look. "Well, can he?"

Pulling the card out of my shirt pocket, I handed it to him. "I wrote down about ten verses on the subject that you can look up in your Bible. Read them sometime and then tell me what you think."

A few days later, he comes back to me with the correct answer!

I could have told him, but instead I gave him the verses and made him do the work. (By the way, if you want the answer to his question, get your concordance!)

My daughter comes to me with a dilemma she is facing in school. She seems to be caught in the middle of a conflict between two girls, both of whom are close friends. I walk over to my bookshelf and pull off a book about relationships, written by an author whom I trust and admire. Flipping to the table of contents, I do a quick check. "Let's get some ideas from this book. Read chapter 4 and then let's talk about it after dinner tonight."

There are many good books on relationships, self-esteem, parenting advice, solving conflicts, etc. Build a good library with the best of these books. This gives you the option of providing your children with a resource in which they can find the answers to their questions. Notice I said, *they* find it.

By now a few of you are screaming in frustration, "Why not just tell them?!?"

Nice try, but by now you know my policy concerning answering questions. I will, however, help you get the wagon rolling a little. If I tell my children a solution to a problem they are facing, they will say, "Dad thinks I should do this..." It is just my opinion. But if I guide them with a few well-directed questions, or narrow their search, or tell a story, or offer a resource that helps them to the right answer, whose opinion does it then become?

Now you're thinking.

Step Six - Praise and Reward
"The wicked worketh a deceitful work: but to him that soweth righteousness shall be a sure reward." Proverbs 11:18

Children respond positively to praise. The best way to reinforce good behavior is through genuine, sincere compliments. As your children develop deductive reasoning and problem solving skills, be sure to praise and reward them.

Step Seven - Purposeful Correction
"The rod and reproof give wisdom, but a child left to himself bringeth his mother to shame." Proverbs 29:15

Be careful when reproving your children when they fail to think through a problem. Most educators will tell you that most children do not develop deductive reasoning skills until they are eight to ten years of age. Until then, it is hard for them to think through a multiple step problem.

The wrong type of rebuke can also be very damaging when dealing with this area of your children's development. They are going to do some dumb things at times! However, never rebuke them by calling them "stupid" or "dumb". Also, never yell or scream at your children. Remember, all correction needs to be purposeful. All correction must contribute to their advancement, to their growth. We are commanded to "bring them up" not "put them down."

The wise in heart shall be called prudent: and the sweetness of the lips increaseth learning. Proverbs 16:21

Part Two
Chapter 6

Clarity of Purpose

To be born, live, then die without finding and fulfilling the purpose for which you were created is to waste your life. The song writer wrote, "Only one life, so soon it will pass, only what's done for Christ will last."

We see in the twelve year old Christ, *clarity of purpose*. At still a tender age, He knew why He was here.

"And he (Jesus) said unto them, How is it that ye sought me? wist ye not that I must be about my Father's business?" Luke 2:49

By the time our children reach the age of twelve, they should be fully aware that they were put here on earth for one main objective -- to accomplish the Father's business. If someone were to ask one of your children, "What do you want to do when you grow up?", wouldn't it be wonderful if, with eyes shining and with a heart full of sincerity he or she would answer, "I want so much to find the purposes for which God has created me, and accomplish those purposes. I want to spend my life doing the will of my Heavenly Father!"

Well, if you dream this for your children, then you can help them by putting a ladder in that dream; a ladder that will cause them to rise above the fleshly, materialistic, selfish goals for existence that seem to have humanity caught in a choke hold; a ladder that will help them to climb high enough to focus on the eternal instead of the temporal. Give them a ladder that will help them find and accomplish the Father's business!

Step One: Proper Evaluation
"Be thou diligent to know the state of thy flocks, and look well to thy herds." Proverbs 27:23

For small children to go through the "I want to be a fireman", then a cowboy, then an astronaut phase -- all this is quite normal and harmless, as long as they are not longing to be something sinful or selfish. However, even when these dreams are expressed by our children, it would be good for our answer to be, "That would be great if that is what God's perfect will is for you."

Evaluate often in which direction your child is leaning. Along with the normal childhood dreams, do they ever express a desire to serve the Lord? I am not just talking about a desire to become a preacher, missionary or evangelist. Do they ever verbally dream of being a Sunday School teacher, a deacon, or a church bus captain? Is the Father's business ever mentioned?

Step Two - Pointed Prayer
"...ye have not, because ye ask not." James 4:4b

There are some prayers that you should pray often in the presence of your children. I still remember the feeling I got every time I heard my dad pray for me by name -- not just praying for "the boys" but praying for me! It would be good if we did this more. Pray for your children by name in their presence and pray that they would find the will of God and accomplish it. They will carry the memory of those prayers for a lifetime.

Step Three - Parental Modeling
"My son, give me thine heart, and let thine eyes observe my ways." Proverbs 23:26

We must stop and ask ourselves, "What do my children see when they 'observe my ways'?" Do they see the Father's business take priority over "the cares of this world and the deceitfulness of riches"? Do I have clarity of purpose?

My friend, there is no more important mission than to find and accomplish the will of God. This is not the pursuit of some distant, one-time event, but a daily, moment-by-moment obedience to the principles of the Bible and the promptings of the Holy Spirit. Do we live for God, or for ourselves? This is paramount, because more than likely our children will follow our example as they live out their lives.

Step Four - Patient Instruction
"My son, hear the instruction of thy father, and forsake not the law of thy mother." Proverbs 1:8

1. Publicly dedicate each of your children to the Lord.

Just the other day, a sweet young couple in our church made their way to the altar during the invitation. In the young mother's arms was a tiny bundle of sleeping joy, a baby girl just over a week old. I met them at the altar, chatted with them a few minutes and then announced to the people that this couple had come to dedicate their child to the Lord. They understood that God had given them this child and now they were giving her back to God. I charged this young couple to dedicate themselves as well, to the rearing of their child to the glory of God. I then led in a dedication prayer. This was a great time of rejoicing, and our people promised to pray for this new addition to our church family.

At many baby dedication services, a small Bible is presented to the child with the date inscribed. Years later, this Bible can be used as a teaching tool, as a prompter that will remind us to again and again tell our children the story of how, from birth, they were dedicated to God to be reared for His glory.

Evangelist Bob Kelly came to our church when I was a teenager. He preached many revivals for our young church in its early years. I will never forget him telling how he and his wife had dedicated each of their children to the Lord when they were first born. They prayed this prayer over each of their young infant girls, "Lord, I give You back this precious life that You have lent to us to rear for Your service. Please Lord, let her grow up to find Your will, to serve You and to live for You. Now Lord, if in Your divine knowledge You see that she will grow up to bring shame and reproach to Your name, we ask, Lord, that You take her home early, before she would be allowed to hurt the testimony of the Lord Jesus. As much as it would break our hearts, we would rather have her safe in Your arms than down here turning others away from the Gospel of Christ."

Wow! Today's generation of parents needs to rediscover this level of determination and dedication when it comes to rearing your children for God! You may feel that you could never pray such a prayer, but I believe this evangelist was right in doing so. He shared this with his three daughters from time to time as they grew. I kept tabs on these girls, and all married Christian men and are serving the Lord faithfully to this day.

2. Teach them that God granted them life and that He formed them from their mother's womb for a specific task.

Besides the Gospel story, this may be one of the most important truths that you can teach to your children. No child is an accident or a mistake! God alone is the Giver of life and He never creates life without assigning that life a divine purpose.

"Then the word of the Lord came unto me saying, Before I formed thee in the belly, I knew thee; and before thou camest forth out of the womb I sanctified thee, and ordained thee a prophet unto the nations." Jeremiah 1:4-5

In these verses, we see the call of Jeremiah, but please notice a great truth that is clearly taught in these Scriptures: Jeremiah was not just *called* to be a prophet, he was *created* to be a prophet! He was formed in his mother's womb to be a prophet, set aside and ordained unto this task before he was born.

In August of 1979, God tapped me on the heart in a Tuesday night revival meeting and called me into the Gospel ministry. Although I look back at that date with reverence, in all honesty, God had decided that I would be a preacher of the Gospel before He gave me the gift of life in my mother's womb. I was not just called to preach in August of 1979, I was created to preach, formed to preach, sanctified to preach, and ordained to preach during the nine months previous to my birth.

I share this with you because God has a perfect will and calling for each of our children -- and it is up to us as parents to help convince them that there is nothing more important than discovering and doing the will of God.

3. Teach your children that there is nothing more important than finding the perfect will of God, and doing it!

It may not be a call to preach, but there is a service to God, a specific church in which to serve, and a specific task or tasks that they have been created to accomplish -- specific people that they have been pre-ordained to win to Christ. To live life without discovering and accomplishing what God placed us on earth to do is to die a failure.

4. Teach your children that they must be willing to surrender their will for God's will.

What if I told you that when Christ was here on earth, He sometimes had a different will than God the Father. You would probably say, "You'll have to prove that!" Okay, keep reading.

"...O my Father, if it be possible, let this cup pass from me: nevertheless not as I will, but as thou wilt." Matthew 26:39b

"And he (Jesus) was withdrawn from them about a stone's cast, and kneeled down, and prayed, saying, Father, if thou be willing, remove this cup from me: nevertheless not my will, but thine be done." Luke 22:41-42

Notice, "not as I will, but as thou wilt." The human side of Jesus would have preferred not to face the suffering that awaited Him. The divine Christ would have preferred not to become sin and be separated from the Father. It should not shock us that Jesus, at times, had a different will than that of the Father. *It is not sin to prefer something other than what is the perfect will of God; it only becomes sin when we are not willing to surrender our will for that of the Father's.*

All of us are, at times, faced with a situation where we want something that is not the Father's will. Often I have stood by the death bed of a dear friend or loved one and prayed for God to heal them. I did not want what God willed. I wanted them restored to health and be given extended years. This is not wrong in itself. But when we refuse to pray at the end of our time of asking, that humble and trusting "nevertheless", then we err.

Growing up, I wanted to become a state policeman. During high school I took steps in that direction, beginning to lay the groundwork for a career in law enforcement. One day an evangelist challenged me to seek the will of God, and be willing to accept it even if it was something other than my will. I struggled with this for awhile, but one night went to an old-fashioned altar and told the Lord, "Nevertheless, not as I will but as thou wilt". A few months later, God called me to preach. It was not a sin to want to be a policeman. It could have become sin had I insisted on my will above that of the Father's.

I say again: we must instill within our children this important truth: to live and die without discovering and accomplishing the purpose for which God created us is to stand before Him one day as a failure!

Step Five - Practical Training
"Train up a child in the way he should go; and when he is old, he will not depart from it." Proverbs 22:6

If your children are to grow up and accomplish the purpose for which they were created, then we need to instill into them these important attributes.

1. Train them to do the revealed will of God.

The revealed will of God is contained in the pages of His Holy Word. After working with young people for over twenty years, I have become convinced of one unequivocal truth: a young person who will not obey the Word of God will also not obey the Spirit of God. If they disobey the written commands, what makes you think that they will obey the quiet promptings of the Spirit as He guides and directs? Train your children to obey the commands of God's Word.

2. Train within your children a quiet Christ-confidence!

My mother's life verse is Philippians 4:13, *"I can do all things through Christ which strengtheneth me."* The good people of our church learned that this was my mother's favorite verse, so they were prone to give her plaques, paintings and porcelain that had this verse inscribed upon them. Pretty soon, you couldn't stand in a room of our home without seeing that verse--I even had to stare at it when I went to the bathroom!

I praise the Lord that God surrounded me with that verse as I grew up. Within me was a quiet confidence, a divine assurance that whatever God would ask of me in life, I could do it with His strength.

I detest the mentality of this "I can't" generation. YES, YOU CAN!!! If God bids you walk on the water, you can by His grace and power. I refuse to accept those two words from our young people.

"Pastor Jerry, I can't get up in front of people. I just can't."

The seventh grade girl in front of me had just transferred from the public school system into our Christian school. Someone there had determined that she belonged in a Learning Disability class. Our diagnostic tests given at the time of her transfer placed her at 5th grade level in Math, Reading and English - a full two years behind her grade level.

She was almost frantic as she showed me the assignment before her.

"It says here that I have to give an oral report. I can't do that!"

I called her by name. "Get out your Bible."

Looking shocked, she slowly retrieved her Bible from her desk.

"Now, turn to Philippians chapter four, verse 13." After a few minutes, she found the verse.

"Read it out loud."

"I can do all things through Christ, which strengtheneth me."

"Now, say that verse to yourself 100 times and I will be back to talk to you about your report." I then turned and walked away to assist another student.

I glanced back over my shoulder to see her sitting there staring at me, looking stunned. I motioned for her to obey my request, and soon looked back to see her counting on her hand as she began to say the verse over and over to herself. When she was finished, I walked back to her desk.

"There is a phrase that we don't use here at Blessed Hope Baptist School. That phrase is 'I can't.' This afternoon, after your other work is completed, I am going to sit down with you and show you how to prepare notes for your oral report. Next Friday, you are going to stand in front of the class and give your report. While you are giving your report, you are going to look only two places: at the notes in front of you, or at me. I will be standing at the back of the class. You can do this with Christ's help."

"But I..." She hesitated, sizing me up. "Yes, sir," she then whispered, still unconvinced.

The next Friday, she stood before the class, visibly shaking. Her voice quivered with each word, but her face wore a look of determination. When she looked up, it was at me and I was nodding my encouragement at every word. When she finished, she almost collapsed in her chair. But she had done it. And on her face was a look of triumph. I said nothing, just smiled.

We encouraged her to set high goals. I watched that young lady finish six years of school curriculum in the next four years. I have never seen anyone try harder in my life. I continued to give her "impossible" things to accomplish and she continued to accomplish them. I could always tell when she was having a particularly rough day. On her bulletin board by her desk would be Philippians 4:13 scribbled on a piece of paper and tacked where she could see it. When she entered her junior year of High School, she had caught up academically with her class. She did it with Christ's help. She did it because she wasn't allowed to say, "I can't."

The day came when she walked across the platform of Blessed Hope Baptist Church to receive her high school diploma. She earned it by completing 46 credits of high school level curriculum, with a 3.25 GPA. Her graduation speech was incredible. It was delivered with poise and grace, sincerity and tears, and the audience was visibly moved. Most there knew of all she had overcome to graduate that night. I closed my eyes and smiled as I remembered the little junior high girl who swore to me she couldn't.

A few days later, my wife and I helped her pack all her earthly belongings into a van and drove her to Louisville, Kentucky. She wanted to spend her summer volunteering at a church camp before enrolling the next fall as a freshman in Bible college. On the trip down, she was excited, but nervous — new environment, new people, new challenges. It would be financially challenging. She would have to work and pray her way through college. Even then, she would need a few miracles now and then.

A part of me asked, "Can she do this?" I had to smile at my doubt. If she knew what I had thought, she would probably have made me get out my Bible and say a certain verse to myself 100 times.

3. Observe the direction of their talents, interests, and personality, then train them "in the way they should go" (or to find the path they are appointed, or the road that is their portion.)

I have observed the two extremes. Some parents are determined that their children go into full-time service for the Lord. The old-time preachers used to have a label for those who surrendered into the ministry because of the pressure exerted upon them from their parents. They called them "mama called and papa sent." These young men never last long in the Lord's work. I have, however, also seen parents just as determined that their children grow up to work in the family business and live a stone's throw down the road. Remember, we are honor-bound to rear our children to accomplish God's will for their lives, not our will for their lives. If that takes them across town or across the ocean, so be it. God's will is all that should matter.

Step Six - Praise and Reward
"The wicked worketh a deceitful work: but to him that soweth righteousness shall be a sure reward." Proverbs 11:18

Brag on your children every time they spend time accomplishing "the Father's business." Encourage them to serve the Lord and praise them for their involvement. Remind them often that you dedicated them to the Lord, but then remind them that this is not enough. They themselves need to surrender their lives fully to the Lord. When God answers your prayers and they make this decision, make a big deal of it!

Also, give them the assurance that they will have your support in whatever God has called them to do. Remind them that you will be proud of them no matter what they grow up to be -- be it a plumber or a preacher -- as long as they know it is the will of God.

Step Seven - Purposeful Correction
"The rod and reproof give wisdom, but a child left to himself bringeth his mother to shame." Proverbs 29:15

I think that children should be gently reproved anytime they proclaim that they have decided what they will be when they grow up. Teach them that God has already decided what they are to be; that He also has created and equipped them to perform this service. Remind them of the importance of finding and accomplishing God's will for their lives, and not to be presumptuous in deciding what that is without a clear leading of the Holy Spirit.

Part Three

The Man and Woman Beside the Manger

Part Three
Chapter 1

There Are No Perfect Parents

"And they came with haste, and found Mary, and Joseph, and the babe lying in a manger." Luke 2:16

We have a fine man in our church who travels the country giving seminars on estate planning at Baptist churches. One of the things he stresses to young couples who have children is the importance of having a will drawn up. One stating your wishes concerning the legal guardianship of your children who are minors in the event that both parents are killed in an accident.

I still remember when my wife and I sat down to discuss this. I mean, if you are not there to rear your children, who would you wish to take your place? What a monumental decision! You would need to have a great deal of confidence, trust and respect for the couple you would choose to rear your child!

God the Father one day had to make that decision. He decided who would rear His Son! That alone gives me a great deal of respect for Mary and Joseph. Of all the couples in Israel, God sought out this young, espoused Jewish couple to become the earthly parents of the Savior of the world. For this fact alone, I think that Mary and Joseph's lives are worthy of a careful study.

First of all, we know that they were not perfect people. Despite what the Catholics and others teach, Mary was not sinless. Both Mary and Joseph, I am sure, made their share of mistakes. They once misplaced their son for three days! I hope that fact alone is of some encouragement to you! Perfection is not a necessary attribute to rear godly children. This book has not been written by a perfect dad. My wife is not a perfect mother. There are no perfect parents, so cut yourself some slack!

I do hope you share with me the desire to be the best parent you can possibly be. Your children deserve that from you. I hope you want to improve and are willing to learn to be better.

I think we can all learn a thing or two from the lives of Mary and Joseph. What attributes do we see that caused them to find "favour with God"? What can we learn as parents from the lives of the couple who were selected to teach and train Jesus from infancy?

Part Three
Chapter 2

Mary, the Mother of Jesus

I believe there are ten outstanding attributes found in the life of Mary as we study her throughout the Scriptures. Here they are!

1. Mary Was a Lady of Moral Integrity

"And in the sixth month the angel Gabriel was sent from God unto a city of Galilee, named Nazareth, to a virgin espoused to a man whose name was Joseph, of the house of David; and the virgin's name was Mary." Luke 1:26-27

Although she was espoused to Joseph -- promised to him and soon to become his wife -- we find that she was a virgin. Our children desperately need to see in their mothers a clear example of moral integrity. Ladies, stay true to your husband. Live out your wedding vows. In your behavior, in your dress standards, and in all your interactions, may there never be a shadow of doubt concerning your virtue! Despite what the world says or thinks, God's standards have not changed. He still regards a woman of moral integrity as one whose "price is far above rubies".

2. Mary Was a Lady Who Secured Divine Favor

"And the angel came in unto her, and said, Hail, thou art highly favoured, the Lord is with thee: blessed art thou among women." Luke 1:28

I often am reminded by the Holy Spirit of the story found in the first chapter of Job. How wonderful that when Satan -- "the accuser of the brethren" -- presented himself before the Lord, God was able to

83

brag on Job. I often think, "If God and Satan were to have the same conversation today concerning me, have I lived in such a way to give God something to brag about to Satan or Satan something to accuse me of before God?"

We need a generation of mothers today who are more concerned with securing God's favor than securing the world's approval! Any mother who follows Bible principles in the rearing of her children will be going against most of what is considered acceptable by this tainted and sinful world system. Make it your goal to secure the favor of God!

3. Mary Was a Submissive Lady

"And Mary said, Behold the handmaid of the Lord; be it unto me according to thy word." Luke 1:38a

Do you not suppose that Mary understood the implications that came with being found with child while still espoused to Joseph? What would Joseph think? What would others say?

All of this mattered not to Mary. God had revealed to her His will, and she submitted to it without question. She considered herself the Lord's handmaid, His servant whose job was to do His bidding, without complaint or hesitation. She willingly and cheerfully lived her life *"according to thy word"*.

In this age of role reversals, women's lib, selfishness and cross-dressing, Mary's example lifts from off the pages of God's Word like sweet, precious ointment. How refreshing to find a young lady who understood that submissiveness was not a sign of weakness, but an attribute of spiritual strength. Selfishness demands to be served! Submissiveness finds greatness in service to God.

4. A Lady of Praise and Worship

"And Mary said, My soul doth magnify the Lord..." Luke 1:46

The *magnificat* that was offered from the lips of Mary to Jehovah God and recorded for our reading in Luke chapter one, may be the purest record of worship and praise that was ever uttered by mortal lips. Filled with human humility and divine adoration, it overflows from the abundance of a heart fixed upon the eternal.

Our children need to hear their mothers praise the Lord. They need to feel the glow of genuine worship. From infancy, they need to look into the eyes of a mother whose eyes are fixed on God. Away with complaining, crying and criticism! For your children's sake, magnify the Lord.

5. A Lady of Meticulous Obedience

"And when the eight days were accomplished for the circumcising of the child, his name was called Jesus, which was so named of the angel before he was conceived in the womb. And when the days of her purification according to the law of Moses were accomplished, they brought him to Jerusalem to present him to the Lord; (As it is written in the law of the Lord, Every male that openeth the womb shall be called holy to the Lord;) And to offer a sacrifice according to that which is said in the law of the Lord, A pair of turtledoves, or two young pigeons." Luke 2:21-24

The angel instructed this young couple what to name the child and they obeyed. The law of Moses contained detailed instruction concerning the days of purification and they were meticulously followed. The law commanded that the firstborn be presented unto the Lord, and again we see Mary complying to its instruction. The law of God specified what was considered an acceptable offering and we see exact obedience. What becomes clear is that both Mary and Joseph believed that it was important to meticulously obey every command and precept of God.

Again and again the Bible repeats the most important instruction God has for children: OBEY! Yet how can they best learn instant and complete obedience? They must see it in their parents. Mary set this example before her Savior Son.

6. Mary Was a Lady of Quiet Contentment

"And she brought forth her first born son, and wrapped him in swaddling clothes, and laid him in a manger; because there was no room for them in the inn." Luke 2:7

"We are going where? Bethlehem? Can't you see I'm pregnant? And I hope you don't expect me to ride that old broken down donkey! You know, if you would work harder, we could have a chariot like the neighbors! And by the way, you still haven't given me any money for new baby clothes. What do you expect me to dress the kid in when it's born, rags?"

"What do you mean they don't have a room! You better find something! You have? OK, where are we staying? A barn!!! You think I'm going to spend the night in a barn with a bunch of smelly animals? I knew I should have listened to my mother and held out for a better husband!"

We cannot in our wildest imagination envision Mary carrying on like this. Instead, we see a quiet contentment, a thankfulness for whatever God has provided. Godliness with contentment did indeed produce for her great gain! She was chosen to deliver to the world the greatest gift it has ever received! Jesus Christ, the anointed One of Israel!

7. Mary Was a Noble Mother
"And when they were come into the house, they saw the young child with Mary his mother..." Matthew 2:11

Ten times in the book of Matthew, Mary is identified as Christ's mother. Twice in Mark, eight times in Luke and nine times in John she is called by this noblest of all titles. Over thirty times in all, the New Testament again and again refers to Mary by calling her "mother." Above all other things in her life, I believe Mary was most blessed being what God had called her to be: a mother!

What has happened to society? Why have we as Christians allowed ourselves to turn our back on God's Holy Word and redefine greatness by the world's standards! Dear lady, if God has allowed you the privilege of being a mother, embrace it as the highest of all callings! The hand that rocks the cradle still rules the world!

Many Christian women are more concerned with climbing the corporate ladder than rearing godly children. There is no greater title than that of "mom". I am fearful that if Christ would have been born in today's society, and placed into many a Christian home, the above verse would read, "And when they were come into the house, they saw the young child with Suzy, his daycare sitter!"

8. Mary Was a Lady of Great Faith
"And it came to pass, that, when Elizabeth heard the salutation of Mary, the babe leaped in her womb; and Elizabeth was filled with the Holy Ghost: And she spake out with a loud voice, and said, Blessed art thou among women and blessed is the fruit of thy womb. And whence is this to me, that the mother of my Lord should come to me? For, lo, as soon as the voice of thy salutation sounded in mine ears, the babe leaped in my womb for joy. And blessed is she that believed: for there

shall be a performance of those things which were told her from the Lord." Luke 1: 41-45

Did you see what Elizabeth said to her? *Blessed is she that believed!* The angel had said to Mary just a few days before this account, "For with God nothing shall be impossible." And Mary believed!

Blessed is the child who has a mother who believes that God is the God of the impossible! I believe that a child who is blessed with a mother of great faith will more than likely grow up to do the impossible for God!

9. Mary Was a Lady Faithful to God's House

"And when they were come in, they went up into an upper room, and John, and Andrew, Philip, and Thomas, Bartholomew, and Matthew, James the son of Alphaeus, and Simon Zelotes, and Judas the brother of James. These all continued with one accord in prayer and supplication, with the women, and Mary the mother of Jesus, and with his brethren." Acts 1:13-14

Where was the first place Mary took Jesus after He was born? To the temple at Jerusalem to be presented unto the Lord. Where did Simeon the priest find the consolation of Israel? *"And he (Simeon) came by the Spirit into the temple: and when the parents brought in the child Jesus, to do for him after the custom of the law, then took he him up in his arms and blessed God..." (Luke 2:27-28).* Where did Mary and Joseph take Jesus each year at the feast of the Passover? The temple. Later when Jesus preached His first sermon in His home town of Nazareth, it is written, *"And he came to Nazareth, where he had been brought up: and, as his custom was, he went into the synagogue on the sabbath day..." (Luke 4:16a).* Who instilled in Him this custom or habit? A faithful mother. Where do we find Mary forty days after watching her Son crucified on Golgotha's hill? We find her in the upper room on the first day of the week, attending an old-fashioned prayer meeting, then ten days later, out soul winning in the streets of Jerusalem on the day of Pentecost.

Mary didn't make excuses when it came to church attendance. She simply got up, got the kids ready, and attended the house of God faithfully. America could see revival in one generation if every mother would see to it that her children were in a Bible-preaching church every Sunday!

10. Mary Was a Lady of Spiritual Meditations

"But Mary kept all these things, and pondered them in her heart." Luke 2:19

This was not some shallow, silly little Jewish girl. There was a depth to Mary, a spiritual maturity that belied her years. She had found to be true what King David her ancestor had penned years before, "But his delight is in the law of the Lord, and in his law doth he meditate day and night." I believe Mary was in the habit of pondering. She was a woman of spiritual meditations. Because of this, she was like "a tree planted by the rivers of water." Her leaves did not wither. She brought forth her fruit in her season, and her *whatsoevers* prospered.

Show me a deeply thoughtful, spiritually grounded mother and I will show you some blessed children! Do not be like the "silly women laden with sin" who run to and fro from house to house, feeding on the hog slop of shallow gossip. Instead, spend much time in spiritual meditation, seeking the mind and heart of God! Ponder the wisdom principles of His Word; you will need them again and again as you rear your children for the Lord's glory and service.

Part Three
Chapter 3

Joseph, Christ's Father Figure

I am a big fan of Joseph's. If I was pressed upon to write down a list of the top ten most remarkable men of the Bible, this carpenter from Nazareth would be on that list. When I meditate upon Joseph's life, the word integrity always comes to mind. Here are ten outstanding attributes of this amazing man selected by God to be the earthly "dad" to Jesus.

1. An Honest, Law-Abiding Man

"And it came to pass in those days, that there went out a decree from Caesar Augustus, that all the world should be taxed... And all went to be taxed, everyone into his own city. And Joseph also went up... To be taxed with Mary, his espoused wife, being great with child." Luke 2:1-5

I am sure that Joseph was as excited about additional taxes being levied against him as we are when it happens to us! The timing was terrible for a required trip to Bethlehem since Mary was in the last weeks of her pregnancy, "great with child". Yet Joseph made the trip. Why? Because he was an honest, law-abiding man.

Has it ever occurred to you that God used this taxation as a means to fulfill the Old Testament prophecy concerning the town where Christ would be born? Men, many times we try to rationalize civil disobedience, but a careful reading of Romans chapter thirteen, verse one reminds us, *"Let every soul be subject to the higher powers. For there is no power but of God: the powers that be are ordained of God. Whosoever therefore resisteth the power, resisteth the ordinance of God: and they that resist shall receive to themselves damnation."*

How important that we set before our family a model of honesty and obedience to God-ordained authorities. God often uses unpopular decisions made by even Godless men to accomplish His will. If the "powers that be" pass a law and it is not contrary to the Word of God, then we should obey that law.

2. A Just Man

"Now the birth of Jesus Christ was on this wise: When as his mother Mary was espoused to Joseph, before they came together, she was found with child of the Holy Ghost. Then Joseph her husband, being a just man, and not willing to make her a publick example, was minded to put her away privily." Matthew 1:18-19

Joseph was a man committed to doing right. I believe in every situation he faced, he asked himself, "What is the just thing to do? What is the right thing to do?" I believe he used the law of God as a basis for what was right. Joseph knew that the law of God condemned immoral behavior. When he found out that Mary was with child, he intended to call off the marriage, because he would not marry a fornicator. In this he was right and just. But as we see, he was also merciful.

3. A Merciful Man

It was well within Joseph's rights to bring Mary before the elders of Israel and have her stoned outside the city for her supposed infidelity. Notice though, that although Joseph was determined to do the just thing, he also chose to carry out justice in the most merciful of manners. To protect Mary and her family from public embarrassment, he was planning to put her away privately.

Gentlemen, there is a great lesson here! Wise Solomon wrote under divine inspiration, *"Let not mercy and truth forsake thee: bind them about thy neck; write them upon the table of thine heart: So shalt thou find favour and good understanding in the sight of God and man." (Proverbs 3:3-4).* Truth without mercy will make you an ogre, but mercy without truth will make you a liberal! Your children need a father who will stand for what is right, but they also need a father who will be generous and merciful within the boundaries of what is right. Always punish sin, but do it in the most gentle way possible that will still accomplish the needed correction in the child's attitude and behavior.

4. Joseph Was A Man of Spiritual Meditations

"But while he thought on these things, behold, the angel of the Lord appeared unto him in a dream, saying, Joseph, thou son of David, fear not to take unto thee Mary thy wife: for that which is conceived in her is of the Holy Ghost." Matthew 1:20

So many times we make mistakes as leaders of our family by simply not taking the time to meditate on a decision. Most major decisions are best made after some time of spiritual consideration. Notice, God's will was revealed to Joseph, *"while he thought on these things."* As I look back at my life, most decisions that I made in haste I afterward regretted. I can picture Joseph, stealing away to a quiet place under the stars, seeking God's leading as he wrestled with what to do. I tell my young adult class that great truths and great thoughts are afraid of crowds. They await a chance to reveal themselves to the one who takes the time to be alone.

5. A Man of Great Faith

"Then Joseph being raised from sleep, did as the angel of the Lord had bidden him, and took unto him his wife." Matthew 1:24

Faith is the willingness to obey the commands of God, even when we do not fully understand where that obedience will lead us.

Joseph simply believed God. A pregnant wife who was still a virgin made no logical sense. But God had spoken and that was enough for this man of simple faith. He would do what "the Lord had bidden him," and he would do it by faith.

Men, let us not be guilty of making hasty decisions. Seek the will of God and wait for clear direction. But when we have received from the Lord an answer, then let us also not be guilty of faithlessness. Step out by faith and obey what God has said to do!

6. A Man of Moral Restraint

"Then Joseph being raised from sleep did as the angel of the Lord had bidden him, and took unto him his wife: And knew her not till she had brought forth her firstborn son: and he called his name Jesus." *Luke 1:24-25*

Joseph took Mary to wife, but exercised moral restraint until after she had given birth to the Savior. God then blessed this young couple with other children, four sons and at least two daughters (Matthew 13:55-56). What I think is worthy to note is that although Joseph had every legal right to consummate the marriage on their wedding day, he did what was right. Jesus would indeed be birthed by a virgin, as the Old Testament Scriptures prophesied it to be.

Gentlemen, compare Joseph's moral restraint and unquestioned integrity to a generation of males who do not even have the decency to live within the clear, moral boundaries clearly defined by God's Word. Physical intimacy is pure and wholesome within the confines of marriage, but sexual relationships before marriage and outside of marriage are condemned by the Scriptures again and again. Paul warned the church of Philippi, "Beware of dogs." How sad it is that we have in society a large portion of the male population that has the moral restraint of a surly, mangy, back-alley hound.

Real men—true men—Godly men learn to exercise moral restraint. Live out your wedding vows. Be true to the *"wife of thy youth" (Proverbs 5:18-23).*

7. An Obedient Man

"Then Joseph, being raised from sleep, did as the angel of the Lord had bidden him..." Matthew 1:25

Four times in the first two chapters of Matthew, we see Joseph receiving clear instruction from the Lord. First, in the above verse when Joseph was instructed to take Mary to wife, and he *"did as the angel of the Lord had bidden him"*.

Secondly, Joseph was warned of God in a dream to take his wife and the young child and flee into Egypt. The Bible says in the verse that follows this warning, *"When he (Joseph) arose, he took the young child and his mother by night, and departed to Egypt" (Matthew 2:14)*. Even the slightest hesitation on Joseph's part could have spelled disaster for his family.

The third time we see God communicating with Joseph, He is instructing him to return to the land of Israel because, *"they are dead that sought the young child's life"* (Matthew 2:20-21). Again, what was Joseph's reaction? *"And he arose, and took the young child and his mother, and came into the land of Israel."*

Lastly, God instructed Joseph to *"turn aside into the parts of Galilee."* And Joseph again obeyed, dwelling in the city of Nazareth (Matthew 2:22-23).

Why do we struggle so much with simple obedience to God? Consider what would have happened if, in each of the four above instances, Joseph had not chosen to obey? Mary would have had to rear Jesus alone. Jesus would have been slain with the other young children of the Bethlehem region. The family would have stayed in Egypt, outside of the will of God. And Jesus would not have been reared in Nazareth, thus causing the Old Testament prophecy, *"He shall be called a Nazarene"*, never to come to pass.

How important it is, men, for us to clearly obey the letter of God's written instruction, and the prompting of the Holy Spirit's leading as we make everyday decisions. Many a Christian man has removed his entire family out of the perfect will of God, simply because he refused to obey God!

8. A Protector and Provider

"And they came with haste, and found Mary, and Joseph, and the babe lying in a manger." Luke 2:16

A wonderful sight awaited the shepherds as they entered the stable that night. They found not only the Christ-child; they found a family. As simple as it may seem, I love this verse because Joseph was there! This was his wife, and the Child God had entrusted into his care, and he was there to be the man, to provide and protect.

As we have already seen, God warned Joseph when his family

was in danger, and it was the his responsibility to take the proper steps to insure their safety. God has ordained that a man be the protector and provider of the family. A man who is too lazy to provide for his family is a disgrace to society. A man who is too cowardly to lay down his life for his family is a disgrace to himself.

9. A Man Who Communicated with God

"But when Herod was dead, behold, an angel of the Lord appeareth in a dream to Joseph in Egypt." Matthew 2:19

As we have already stated, Joseph was a man who communicated often with God. Like Enoch of old, Joseph walked with the Lord. Christ was placed in a family where there was a father who knew how to walk with God.

Paul, the veteran missionary, instructed the young preacher Timothy to teach his men to pray. *"I will therefore that men pray every where, lifting up holy hands, without wrath and doubting." (Titus 2:8)* Every family needs at its helm a man who knows how to get a hold of God. My dear brother, walk with God! Spend much time in the Bible hearing what God has to say to you, and much time on your knees, saying what you need to say to God.

10. A Hard-Working Man

"Is not this the carpenter's son? is not his mother called Mary?" Matthew 13:55

Joseph was not only a hard worker, he was a skilled craftsman. He was a carpenter in the days before power tools. With steady, calloused hands, he carefully crafted carts and cabinets. He lifted, levered, and leveled with biceps knotted with the strength of hard labor. This industrious man was remembered by the people of Nazareth by a simple title that encompassed his strength, his skill and his stamina -- he was to them, "the carpenter."

I thank the Lord that my father did not tolerate laziness in our home. By both example and instruction, he taught us to work hard and to be industrious. Hard work has always been synonymous with manhood. America was a nation built by hard work, and there is little wrong with her that could not be cured by hard work. Let's not rob the next generation by failing to set before our children the example of hard work.

Part Three
Chapter Four

Jesus Loves the Little Children

As I read the four Gospels, there are many times that I wish I had a time machine. I could then travel back and experience first hand what I am reading. If such an opportunity were allowed, high on my list of events to revisit would be a wonderful, intimate scene between Jesus and a group of young children. Does any story better give us a glimpse into the heart of the God-man? Read carefully these selected verses then consider with me some amazing truths about Jesus and little children.

"And they brought young children to him, that he should touch them: and his disciples rebuked those that brought them. But when Jesus saw it, he was much displeased, and said unto them, Suffer the little children to come unto me, and forbid them not: for of such is the kingdom of God.... And he took them up in his arms, put his hand upon them, and blessed them." Mark 10:13-16

I think Jesus never forgot what it was like to be a child. God could have sent Jesus down from Heaven, descending from the clouds as a grown man to come and die for the sins of mankind. But He didn't. He sent Him as a baby, born in a manger. He grew up and experienced infancy, adolescence, and those wonderful and frustrating teenage years. He was "touched with the feelings of our infirmities...yet without sin." He never forgot what it was to be a child.

Jesus took time for children. To Him they were not a bother. He did not treat them as if they were unworthy of His time and attention. As a matter of fact, He was "much displeased" when He saw His disciples trying to shoo them away. He rebuked His disciples and stopped what He was doing to spend time with these young children.

Jesus picked them up and held them. I can almost picture this. Of all the scenes of the greatness of Christ, this to me is one of the most powerful. Little children need to be held. They need to be hugged, kissed, wrestled with, and given piggyback rides. They need the bonding and security that the arms of loving parents and relatives provide.

Jesus blessed them as He held them in His arms. He said something to each of them. Perhaps He prayed for them. Maybe He whispered words of encouragement, some expression of love, or a single piece of divine wisdom. What an example for us! How damaging for children to always hear our words of disapproval, but never to hear us praise them and bless them!

The simplest songs often contain the most important truths. Jesus loved us enough to give us a window into His childhood years. And, as we grew up singing, He has loved all the children since.

Jesus loves the little children,
all the children of the world.
Red and yellow, black and white,
they are precious in His sight.
Jesus loves the little children of the world.

About the Author

With the writing of this book, Pastor Jerry Ross celebrates thirty-three years of Gospel preaching. He is the senior pastor of the Blessed Hope Baptist Church of Jasonville, Indiana, an author, and a Bible conference speaker.

Other Titles by the Author

The Childhood Years of Jesus Christ
The Teenage Years of Jesus Christ
Stay in the Castle
The Seven Royal Laws of Courtship
Is Your Youth Group Dead or Alive?
Grace Will Lead Me Home
The 21 Tenets of Biblical Masculinity
The 21 Tenets of Biblical Femininity (Jerry & Sheryl Ross)
Developing a Teen Soul Winning Program
How to Put on a Parent's Appreciation Night

Soon to be Released by the Author

104 Teen Training Hour Lessons
104 MORE Teen Training Hour Lessons

www.stayinthecastle.com

Ultimate Goal Publications
Jasonville, Indiana